A Manual of Mineralogy

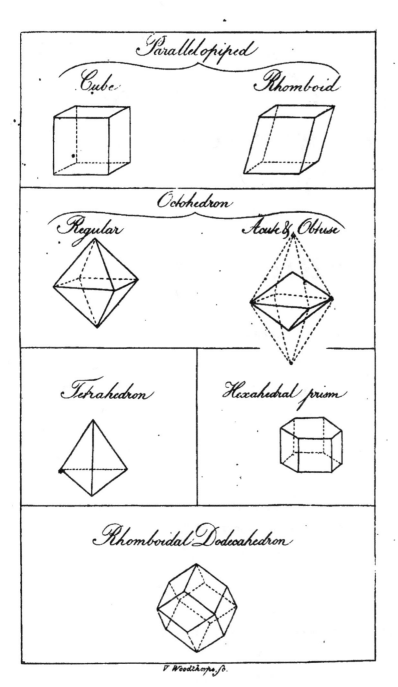

Parallelopiped

Cube

Rhomboid

Octohedron

Regular

Acute & Obtuse

Tetrahedron

Hexahedral prism

Rhomboidal Dodecahedron

V Woodthorpe. sc.

Published by W. POLYBLANK High Cross Truro.

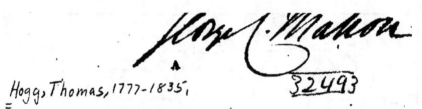

A

MANUAL

OF

MINERALOGY;

IN WICH IS SHOWN HOW MUCH

CORNWALL

CONTRIBUTES TO THE ILLUSTRATION OF THE SCIENCE.

―――

" Hic fontes Natura novos emisit."

―――

TRURO:

PRINTED AND PUBLISHED BY W. POLYBLANK, HIGH CROSS; SOLD
BY G. B. WHITTAKER, LONDON; J. TREGONING,
AND MRS. HEARD, BOOKSELLERS, TRURO.

1825.

ADVERTISEMENT.

This *MANUAL* contains a concise description of minerals in general, and the localities of those of Cornwall, hitherto known, in particular, with the economical uses of the metals, and other species; an account of the mode of smelting tin and copper-ores; an explanation of terms; and mineralogical questions.

A plate of the primary forms, from which the various crystalline modifications proceed, and several new analyses of the mineral productions of the county, are also given.

As a safeguard to faithful description, the author has received liberal assistance. He particularly acknowledges the disinterested kindness of a friend who, as an accurate analyst, is superior to many, and surpassed by few.

The condensed explanations, which are interspersed, are merely intended to render the study more engaging, and to show how short the distance is between mineralogy and a far wider field of science.

The classification is the most simple that could be devised. By avoiding prolixity of definition the author aims at practical utility, that those, who take pleasure in the science, but whom occupation prevents from prosecuting it to any great length, may find its elements clear, and easy of acquirement; and he, respectfully, lays before the public the first Book ever printed in Cornwall on the most beautiful branch of natural history.

August, 1825.

CONTENTS.

INTRODUCTION.

I. THE terrible struggle which nature underwent, before she assumed her present form; her primitive depositions; and those tremendous convulsions, amidst which, subsequent formations were heaved, to imprint beauty, grandeur, and sublimity, on her surface, have given rise to splendid theories, and continue to excite lofty speculations.

Man, while he measures the orbits of celestial worlds, cannot penetrate the veil which wraps the structure of his own globe. Shrouded in impenetrable secrecy, phenomena behold hypothesis, after hypothesis, make its gaudy and transient appearance, and then disappear for ever. Feeble mortal! " Canst thou by searching find out God?" An antient christian writer has said, " *Si scirem, essem ipse Deus.*"

B

The mountains rise; the rivers flow; the
ocean rolls; and it is consistent with the
dignity of the human mind to contemplate
the scene. So we may innocently endeavour to ascertain the nature of the rocks,
and the position of the strata, which constitute the surface of the earth; and, although
it is vain to speculate about the origin of
the world, we may, without the imputation of
rashness, nay we may, with a commendable
curiosity, endeavour to obtain a glimpse of
the antient formation of things.

Powerful chemical agents, present, or
employed, during the operations of creation,
if we may so speak, after having seen the
globe lifted from chaos, at the fiat of omni-
potence, seem to have become condensed.
Embodied in the congealed fluids, or arranged according to their affinities in solid
lava, divested of activity, they lie dormant
in scattered portions of the globe. When
roused from its sleep, by the awakening
touch of science, the liberated captive leaps
forth, destroying, in its escape, the walls of
its silent abode.

These imprisoned agents are more nume-
rously crowded together in Cornwall than in
any other part of the British empire. In a
Geological point of view, that district is
superior to any part of Great Britain; as in

a Mineralogical, it is the most instructive and interesting. From its appearance, a general inference may be drawn of the crust of the earth. We have here an epitome of the structure of the globe.

II. The basis of Cornwall, whether a crystallization arising from fire, or a chrystalline deposite from a watery solution, is granite. It is unstratified; and its masses are the lowest visible layer, surrounding the inner and unknown parts of the county. It presents an undulating surface. Had the ocean not been forced out of the hollows by the progressive accumulation of subsequent formations, the granite eminences would have stood above the surface, as islands, or insulated rocks.

Although petrifactions do not occur in Cornwall, it is from them we chiefly gain our geological knowledge. They are found in other countries in the strata above the granite.

These fossils seem as if they had been deposited amidst oceans of mortar, in a season of tranquillity; to have been lifted, broken, and floated, by tremendous agents. Shells of the most delicate texture, which the first shock of a stormy sea would have crushed; and tender leaves, which a single nip of frost would have shrivelled, are the archives where nature records the revolutions of the globe. They present an imperishable monument of the great catastrophe. By them we know that forests waved, and waters were peopled with fish, before the earth, we tread, obeyed the sun.

The cliffs at the Land's End, resisting the ocean, and exhibiting, amidst everlasting uproar, a scene of magnificent confusion; and the abrupt, vertical, masses, rising every where over the contiguous promon- tory, are granite.

Are these the debris of antient hills?—the scattered remains of degraded mountains?— are the quartz fragments, with which the plains are strewed, the shivered memorials of the veins which intersected them?—

The upper part of St Michael's Mount, Tregoning, Godolphin, Breage, and Carn Bre hills, are links of the granite chain, which geologists trace to Dartmoor.

The granite ridge, which does not exceed three miles in breadth, increases in altitude as it advances eastward. Cape Cornwall rises 229 feet, Carn Bre 697, Brown Willy 1368, and Rippentor 1549, above the level of the sea.

Halfway between Bodmin and Launceston, the granite range becomes greatly widened, or else another tract crosses it nearly at right angles, forming the highest ground in Cornwall.

III. The killas of Cornwall is clay slate of the hardest degree. It is composed of comminuted fragments, which must have existed in another state, prior to their present arrangement. That, adjoining the granite, becomes of a finer grain, as if from resistance before, and pressure behind; it does not split into laminæ: That, resting immediately on the granite, is still more compact; and, under the hammer, it acquires toughness.

On the north and south side of the granite ridge it descends to an unknown depth; and the dip, on the respective sides, is north, and south.—On each side of the cross range, between Bodmin and Launceston, the killas dips east and west. This superincumbent matter has been floated and heaved, at random, like masses of disruptured ice, till it was stopped by the mountain sides of the previouly fixed granite.

At the farthest distance, where the land permits inspection, the argillaceous strata, from the resistance having become diminished appear horizontal.

At St. Michael's Mount, ramifications of

B 3

granite shoot into the killas; and the latter is frequently seen penetrating the granite. This proves that both rocks were in a soft state when they came in contact; or the vein must have been fluid and the rock in that state expressed by the latin word *lentus,* that is, between a solid and a fluid.

The extremity of the county, on the north west and south of St Agnes hill, is killas, which goes inland about 150 fathoms, and extends from Towan-Porth to Seal-Hole mine. Between this and the hill is a tract of granite; Huel Coates mine, lying north west of the hill, is in it; and it, as ascertained by the workings, extends in breath, about 200 fathoms. This granite ridge stands perpendicularly between the killas ranges;—it appears east of Seal-Hole mine, —is lost in the sea, and rises again at Cleggo Point, assuming an easterly direction.*

At Cleggo Point, stupenduous rocks of granite interlie killas; and on as grand a scale, the latter interlies the former. The north and south sides of the cliffs are perpendicular masses of granite, in-

* It is supposed that this granite ridge runs nearly due east towards the Blue-Anchor, where it again breaks out. Hence it may join the great chain which runs along the county. The granite about St. Agnes is called by the miners " bastard granite." and more generally " elvan."—The felspar is mealy, and many blocks may be seen from which it has been weathered out, and which appear as if perforated by worms: the mica generally has disappeared, and the whole degenerates from the granite at Cleggo Point.

termixed with hornstone porphyry, and
they are bounded by clay-slate. Immediately, when beginning to descend the
difficult pass to the shore below, an experienced miner shewed the author, granite
which had been cut; and he added, that by
driving a level a few fathoms southward,
the granite would be perforated, and killas
would be found.

These anomalies have staggered some
geologists; silenced others; and instruct all
not to be too precipitate in their first perusal
of the page of nature, especially in a pro-
vince where every character breathes science.
No man can say whether the claim to prio-
rity of deposition, in these places, is to be
granted to granite or killas.

To the solid superincumbent strata upon
the granite, generally, Cornwall owes that
continuous extent of surface, on which life
and vegetation exist; and in which the in-
dustrious miner finds those mineral treasures
which have, during the lapse of ages,
stamped consideration on the whole land.

IV. The direction of the tin and copper
lodes is always east and west. They are
situated in killas, at no great distance from
the granite range. They are seldom sought
for any where else by cautious adventurers,

The underlie, or deflection from the perpendicular, is north or south. If the north side of the roof of a church, were, retaining its slanting position, supposed to be under ground, it will give an·idea of a lode. In deep mines the lode sometimes passes through the killas, and is continued in granite. There, tin and copper ores are frequently found. The extent of a metallic vein, east and west, has not been ascertained, neither has the depth been fathomed.

Some veins run quite across these, which are called "cross lodes." They are generally barren of tin or copper, but have been found to contain lead, and cobalt, and silver. Their deviation from the perpendicular is east, or west.

When working a rich vein, the miner will find it, on a sudden, disappear. This interruption, to which lodes are liable, is called a *heave*, which is a reverse term for subsidence. This is caused by the cross lodes, which, whenever they intersect a vein, frequently alter its position, so that the vein on the west side of the cross course lies further north than that on the east side.

A cross lode in Huel Peever, about three miles east from Redruth, extends from sea to sea. On its west side, every vein it passes is heaved 50 fathoms farther north from the line it would have otherwise pursued, and which the other part still keeps. It was not until after a search of forty years, that this heaved lode was discovered.

The beautiful crystals, with which the lodes abound, seem—if an opinion may be risked—to have sprung like transparent jelly, from the consolidating mass, and to have coagulated instantaneously. Thus gelatinized, they have ever since, without increase, or diminution, preserved their form, their lustre, and their native purity; and, if undisturbed, will, without liability to change, continue so to the end of time.

Ores of a certain character produce the same metal.—The miner, from experience, can immediately say what ore contains copper; what, tin; and what, lead.

Similar compounds invariably present a similar crystallization; and as the like constituents, without exception produce corresponding prisms, a student in mineralogy having once known a crystal—and such knowledge fills Cornwall with self-taught geometricians—will find no difficulty in ascertaining to what species another of like character belongs.

V. The vast quantity of alluvial matter derived from the breaking up of rocks, and deposited in many vales; gigantic fragments which the impetuous rush of waters could not tumble far from the foundation of the parent hill; pebbles of indestrustible materials rolled to a greater distance; huge blocks of granite piled on each other, with a regularity not inferior to planned masonry, or heaped together in magnificent confusion, stand as monuments of general destruction, and exhibit vestiges of astonishing degradation in Cornwall.

Man contemplates, with solemnity, the wreck of nature, and feels, as he walks amongst her ruins, that the scenery around him occupies the place of more antient formations.

Silicious pebbles, of an oval form, accumulated in heaps, unmixed with any others; or appearing as stripes in the alluvial depositions approaching the shore, seem to have been veins—perhaps, of argillaceous slate. The quartz, from its superior tenacity resisisted decomposition, while the softer part of the rock fell reduced and was carried away. Strewed into millions of angular fragments, disgorged from the suffocated vortex, or splintered from those doomed to the trial of enormous friction, these stones lie drifted over the county, without any other attrition than that to which they

were subjected when washed from their native hills. Again, the amazing deposits of
rolled tin pebbles in the stream works prove
the destruction of neighbouring mountains.
In Carnon Vale, 36 feet below an over-
burthen of granitic gravel and mud, these
pebbles are found mixed with silicious
matter, the debris of the surrounding hills.
From their smooth roundness, and from the
vast quantity deposited, the lodes which
furnished them must have occupied a tract
of country, distant, and extensive.

Pentuan Vale is filled with six alluvial
beds, extending in depth, about 60 feet.
Some of these consist of mud, and marine
sand; others of comminuted granite, which
has been washed down from the north hills.
Roach Rock evidently owes its preservation
to its schorelous composition, which resisted
the overwhelming impetuosity of the delu-
vian waters. In other strata, have been found
shells, leaves of aquatic plants, hazel nuts,
horns of deer, human skulls, branches of
trees, some inclining, some erect, with their
roots fixed in the soil where they grew. Below all these, is the tin ground, full of rolled
pebbles. The mighty torrents whilst pushing
their descent through the immense desola-
tion, formed artificial excavations, which
adorn so much of our rural landscape; and

in them, as an advantageous aperture, the streams of water have chosen their beds, and continue through a varied line of beauty to pursue their way into the sea.

Of all the tin works in Cornwall, to the natural historian, Pentuan is the most attractive. In the moralist it may raise serious reflections.

Among the solitude of these trees, philosophers, perhaps, passed a life of calm repose and contemplation; perhaps the venerable patriarch gave lessons of wisdom, and taught, that the silent grove, the stupendous mountain, the verdant meadow, the spangled canopy of heaven, the vast amphitheatre of nature, were temples of the Divinity; when the fine imagery of rural scenes and all the touching aspect of smiling creation, were, with their inhabitants, swept away by the overwhelming flood, and deposited promiscuously in this chaotic vale.

The Metals at present known are twenty-eight.* Twelve are malleable, viz,

Platinum.
Gold.
Mercury.
Lead.
Palladium.
Silver.
Copper.
Cadmium.
Nickel.
Iron.
Tin.
Zinc.

The other seventeen are brittle, viz,

Osmium.
Iridium.
Rhodium.
Tungsten.
Bismuth.
Uranium.
Cobalt.
Arsenic.
Molybdena.
Tellurium.
Antimony.
Manganese.
Columbium.
Chromium.
Cerium.
Titanium.
Selenium.

* The lately-discovered metals, which form, with oxygen, the alkaline and earthy bases, are omitted. They are noticed in the course of the work.

The acids which are found combined with metallic minerals are eight, viz,

The Sulphuric,
The Muriatic,
The Phosphoric,
The Arsenic,
The Carbonic,
The Chromic,
The Tungstic,
The Molybdic, acids.

Mercury occurs native, and combined with the sulphuric, and muriatic acids. Mineralized by sulphur, it forms Cinnabar its most abundant ore.

Silver occurs native, is found mineralized by sulphur and arsenic, and combined with the sulphuric, muriatic, and carbonic, acids.

Bismuth is found native, and mineralized by sulphur, and its oxide is combined with carbonic acid.

Copper occurs native, and is mineralized by sulphur, and its oxide combined with the sulphuric, muriatic, phosphoric, carbonic, and arsenic, acids.

Iron is found mineralized by sulphur and arsenic, and its oxide combined with the sulphuric, muriatic, phosphoric, carbonic, arsenic, chromic, and tungstic, acids.

Cobalt is mineralized by sulphur and arsenic, and combined with the sulphuric, and arsenic, acids.

Lead is mineralized by sulphur, and its oxide combined with the sulphuric, muriatic phosphoric, carbonic, arsenic, molybdic, and chromic, acids.

Antimony is mineralized by sulphur, and arsenic.

Uranium is found in a state of oxide, and combined with phosphoric acid.

Zinc is mineralized by sulphur, and its oxide combined with the sulphuric, and carbonic, acids.

Manganese is mineralized by sulphur, and its oxide combined with the phosphoric, and carbonic, acids.

Chromium exists as an oxide, or an acid; united with the oxide of lead, it forms chromate of lead; with that of iron, the chromate of iron, from either of which it is extracted.

CRYSTALLIZATION.

In nature, the same body would always concrete in the same crystalline forms, were they not liable to many modifications, which produce dissimilar crystals. Thus, lending itself to different transformations carbonate of lime assumes the form of a rhomboïd, a hexahedral prism, or a dodecahedron. Again, different minerals present the same form. Sulphuret of lead, fluate of lime, sulphuret of iron, and muriate of soda, crystallize in cubes; and sometimes assume the form of a regular octahedron.

The most simple form is regarded as the primary; by following its truncations through a series of gradation, the transitions from the original can be determined to the remotest modification. However diversified the crystals, mechanical division proves that the primitive form, relative to the whole species of the same substance, is invariable; and, to it, crystallographers refer every other geometrical figure it may exhibit.

From a cube of fluate of lime, an octahedron is extracted, by dividing the cube upon its eight solid angles, which discover eight equilateral triangles; hence, we say, the octahedron is the primary form of fluor, and the cube, its secondary.

By striking off the solid angles of an octahedron of galena, we obtain a perfect cube, the angles of which are in the centre of the octahedral planes; hence, the cube is considered the parent nucleus of sulphureted lead, and the octahedron a derivative.

The imagination, when contemplating the delicate architecture of nature, labours in vain to conceive the nucleus as composed of geometrical solids, imperceptible, infinite,—*omni ingenio altiora.*

The primary forms are five, viz, crystals contained within six planes, as the cube and the parallelopipedon; the tetrahedron; the octahedron; the regular hexahedral prism; and the dodecahedron.

The tetrahedron is the simplest of the pyramids; the triangular prism the simplest of the prisms, and the parallelopipedon the simplest of the solids, which have their faces parallel.

The regular octahedron is the most general crystal. It resembles two four-sided pyramids united base to base; the planes are equilateral triangles; and the common base of the two pyramids is a square. This form may be converted into a tetrahedron by the removal of four smaller tetrahedrons from its solid angles; hence, it is not easy to determine, which of these forms is the original, from which their modifications are derived.

The primary forms are thus briefly exemplified;

That of {

Arseniate of iron }
Iron pyrites } is a cube.
Galena }

Grey copper is a tetrahedron.

Red oxide of copper }
Copper pyrites } is an octahedron.
Fluate of lime }

Arseniate of Lead is a regular hexagonal prism.

Garnet }
Blende } is a dodecahedron.

SPECIFIC GRAVITY.

A cubic foot of distilled water weighs 1000 ounces avoirdupois; and from this standard all the respective gravities are taken. A body counterpoised by weights in the hydrostatic balance, will, when immersed in water, lose its equilibrium. To restore this, weight must be added; and that weight will be equal to the weight of a quantity of water as big as the immersed body. A guinea suspended in air is counterbalanced by 129 grains: immersed in water, it requires $7\frac{1}{4}$ to restore the equipoise; and shews, that a quantity of water equal in bulk with the guinea, weighs $7\frac{1}{4}$ grains, or 7,25.—Divide 129, the weight of the guinea, by this, and the quotient will be 17,793, which shews, that the guinea is that number of times as heavy as its bulk of water. In other words, gold weighs about 18 times heavier than the water that would run over the edge of a vessel quite full, on dropping a piece of gold into it. If gold be less than 17, it is too much alloyed; if the quotient be 19, it is fine.

c

Bodies are specifically heavier as they are more dense. If a piece of metal weigh, in air, 72 grains, and nine grains be necessary to restore its equilibrium when weighed in water, 72, divided by 9, gives 8, then the specific gravity is 8, as of copper; that is, copper is 8 times heavier than water.

The metallic minerals are arranged in the following pages, according to the specific gravity of the respective metals, viz.

1 Platinum............................ 28
2 Gold............................... 19
3 Osmium and Iridium alloyed 19
4 Tungsten 17.4
5 Mercury........................ 13.6
6 Lead............................. 11.35
7 Palladium....................... 11.8
8 Rhodium......................... 11
9 Silver............................ 10.50
10 Bismuth......................... 9.88
11 Uranium....................... 9
12 Copper......................... 8.9
13 Cadmium........................ 8.6
14 Nickel.......................... 8.4
15 Cobalt.......................... 8
16 Arsenic......................... 8.35
17 Iron............................ 7.7
18 Tin............................. 7.29
19 Molybdena...................... 7.4
20 Antimony....................... 6.70
21 Tellurium...................... 6.11
22 Zinc........................... 6.9
23 Manganese...................... 6.8
24 Columbium...................... 5.90
25 Chromium....................... 5.90
26 Cerium......................... 4.98
27 Titanium....................... 4.42
28 Selenium....................... 4.3

METALLIC MINERALS.

I. PLATINUM.

Platinum.—It was first brought to England from South America, in 1741. It is of a light steel grey colour; in small flat grains, shining and of a metallic lustre. In this state it is exceedingly impure, containing either in combination, or mechanically mixed, several other metals.

It is one of the most infusible of all the metals. It is reduced in conjunction with arsenic. Refined platinum is the heaviest body in nature. Welding, or adhesion by hammering, in a white heat, is peculiar to iron and platinum. It is soluble in nitro-muriatic acid. Of all metals it expands the least by heat, and resists most agents; hence, it is used for pendulums, pyrometers, watch-wheels, chemical vessels, and speculums for telescopes, in which, from its density, it augments the reflecting power.

II. GOLD.

Gold.—The original form of its crystals is a cube. It does not combine with mineralizing substances. It has no attraction for sulphur, and very little for arsenic. It remains unalterable in the hotest furnace. Aqua regia, (or nitro-muriatic acid,) is its usual solvent.

It has been found in some of the stream-works of Cornwall, and no where else in the county. It most commonly occurs in grains. A quantity of stream tin-ore was found at Treworda, Kenwyn, a good deal of which is still preserved, containing very many grains. To these vales there is reason to believe that the gold was brought down from mountains, with the tin, by long continued floods. The higher up the country they are found, the grains generally are rougher; those farthest down are evidently smoothed by attrition. These rolled tin pebbles and gold are the relics of mountains which have been deposited on mountains which are washed away; and are proofs of the great antiquity of the globe. There is a piece of gold in a matrix of quartz, from Carnon Vale, in the Royal Institution of Cornwall, weighing 11dwts. 6grs.

Graphic Gold consists of tellurium 60, gold 30, silver 10. It burns with a green flame before the blow-pipe. It occurs usually in small six-sided prismatic crystals, in rows which resemble a line of written persepolitan characters. It is of a grey colour.

Electrum ;—Argentiferous Gold. It consists of gold 64, silver 36. Its colour is between that of brass and silver. It is not soluble in nitric or nitro-muriatic acid.

Uses of Gold.—It is softer than any other metal, except lead; it therefore requires an alloy to harden it for most uses.

Standard Gold consists of 11 dwts. and 1 of copper: twelve ounces of this are coined into 44½ guineas.

A little nitric acid applied to the touch stone, *(Lapis Lydius)*, will destroy the traces of all metals, except Gold.

Add to the solution of gold about three times its quantity of sulphuric ether, which will take up the nitro-muriate, leaving the acid colourless at the bottom, which must then be drawn off. Steel dipped into the etherial solution, and instantly washed with clean water, will be completely and beautifully covered with gold.

When a piece of silk dipped in a solution of gold in nitro-muriatic acid is exposed to hydrogen gas, while moist, the gold is instantly reduced.

Copper buttons are dipped into nitric acid, burnished, put into a nitric solution of mercury, stirred until they become white; then put into an amalgam of gold and mercury, with diluted nitric acid, when the gold attaches itself to their surface. They are heated till the mercury begins to run; thrown into a cap of coarse wool, and stirred with a brush. The mercury is then volatilized over the fire. A gross of buttons of one inch diameter, ought, by Act of Parliament, to have five grains of gold on them.

Gold beaters hammer thin rolled plates between skins. One grain is made to cover nearly 57 square inches. They add 3 grains of copper in the ounce, otherwise from its ductility it would pass round the irregularities of the skins and not cover them.

Gold leaf ground with honey, or gum-water, boiled till sufficiently fine, and the honey or gum washed off, is *shell gold* for painting.

Silver is *gilded* with leaves of gold. A rod of this silver drawn into wire and flattened may have 100 square inches covered with one grain of gold.

Burnt rags which had been dipped in a solution of aqua regia, are rubbed with a wet cork, superficially charred, on silver, it is then burnished.

The wire used by lace-makers is drawn from an ingot of silver, previously gilded. From the known diameter and length of the wire, and the quantity of the gold used, it is computed that the covering of gold is only one 12th of the thickness of gold leaf; which is so light as to fly in the air.

Or-moulu is made by rubbing mercury on a thin piece of gold till it becomes paste which is spread on copper; it is then heated to discharge the mercury, and then burnished.

III. OSMIUM AND IRIDIUM.

Osmium and Iridium.—The natural alloy of these occur in small flattened grains, of a metallic lustre, but paler than those of platinum; they were discovered with black powder left after the dissolving of platinum. They are found among the grains of crude platinum, distinguishable by their insolubility in nitro-muriatic-acid; they are not in the least malleable.

IV. TUNGSTEN.

Tungsten consists of acid of tungsten 75, 25. Lime 16, 70. Silex 1, 56, with traces of oxide of manganese, and oxide of iron. It has been found with tin-stone, from which it is distinguished by its greater weight and hardness, and by becoming yellow in nitric acid. It is crystallized in an acute octahedron, which passes, by the truncation of its edges, to a less acute octahedron; and this is sometimes deeply truncated on the summit as to form a four sided table, with the terminal planes bevelled. The lustre is resinous, and sometimes adamantine. With borax before the blowpipe it forms a white glass. (See *Tungstate* of Lime.) The metal tungsten is obtained from the tungstate of lime and from wolfram: it is of a greyish-white, or iron colour, brilliant, hard, and brittle; it is insoluble in the acids. The oxide gives permanence to vegetable colours.

V. MERCURY.

Mercury, besides being found native, is combined with the *sulphuric* and *muriatic* acids, forming *muriate of mercury*: mineralized by sulphur it forms *cinnabar*, its most abundant ore; and with silver, it forms *native amalgam*.

1. *Native Mercury. Hydrargyrum nativum.* It contains no intermixture of any other metal, and is found in most mercurial mines. It does not unite with iron, arsenic, or platinum. It acts spontaneously on gold, silver, lead, tin, bismuth, zinc, and osmium, and, if applied in sufficient quantity, completely dissolves them. It remains fluid in the air, which no other metal does. By a cold below 39 of Fahrenheit's scale, it becomes solid, and may be extended under the hammer without breaking.

By heat, which fixes other metals, it can be volatilized in almost invisible vapour; hence, the pernicious effects experienced by workers in mercury. It is soluble in nitric acid. When contaminated with other metallic bodies, it is purified by distillation.

2.—*Native Muriate of mercury.* It consists of oxide of mercury 76, muriatic acid 16, sulphuric acid 7. It is grey, is faintly translucent, and has an adamantine lustre. The crystals are small rectangular four-sided prisms, terminated by four-sided rhomboidal summits. It is totally volatilized before the blow-pipe, and emits a garlic smell.

3.—*Cinnabar. Sulphuret of mercury.* The mineral is red, steel grey, &c. It gives a scarlet streak. It is sometimes crystallized in obtuse rhombs, six-sided tables, six-sided prisms, tetrahedrons and octahedrons. The pure metal frequently is found disseminated in the sulpheret in fluid globules.

The greatest part of the mercury of commerce is obtained from cinnabar, which yields about 80 per cent. of metal, and 20 of sulphur. The mines of Idria have been long abundant in this mineral. Besides being united with sulphur, it is found mixed with iron and other matter, which gives it a different appearance, as

Hepatic Cinnabar, of which there are two varieties, viz: 1. *Compact*, between cochineal red and lead grey. It consists of mercury 81, sulphur 13, carbon 2, with small proportions of silex, alumine, oxide of iron, copper, and water. It gives a cochineal trace to the *touch-stone.* 2. *Slaty*, a little redder than the former; when exposed to the air, it acquires a liver-brown tint; hence the name, "hepatic," or "liver-ore."

Native Amalgam.—Quicksilver alloyed with silver. The primary form of its crystals, a small dodecahedron.—It consists of silver 36, mercury 64. The mercury before the blow-pipe evaporates and leaves the silver pure.

Uses of Mercury.—Glass is *silvered*, by spreading mercury over tin-foil: when they are united, a plate of glass is slid over to sweep off the superfluous metal. Weights are laid, and the tin becomes cemented to the glass. Two ounces of mercury will silver three square feet of glass.

Hollow *Glass Globes* are silvered by one part of bismuth, one half of lead—the same of pure tin, and two parts of mercury. The solids are fused, and when nearly cold, the mercury is added. The amalgam is poured into the globe; it sticks to the glass, which, by proper motion, becomes silvered completely.

Mercury is used for *collecting gasses* absorbable in water; in the constructions of *thermometers* and *barometers;* and mixed with zinc, it forms an amalgam for *electrical machines.* Combined with the muriatic acid, it forms corrosive *sublimate* Silver, brass, or copper, are gilded thus:—Eight parts of mercury and one of gold are heated in a crucible. As soon as the gold is dissolved, the mixture is poured into cold water, and it is then ready for use. The metal to receive it is brushed over with diluted nitric acid.

VI. LEAD.

Lead, which has never been found native, is combined with *oxygen,* the *sulphuric, muriatic, phosphoric, carbonic, chromic, arsenic,* and the *molybdic*, acids, and alloyed by *sulphur*, forming

$$\left.\begin{array}{l} \textit{Oxide} \\ \textit{Sulphate} \\ \textit{Muriate} \\ \textit{Phosphate} \\ \textit{Carbonate} \\ \textit{Chromate} \\ \textit{Arseniate} \\ \textit{Molybdate} \\ \textit{Sulphuret} \end{array}\right\} \textit{of Lead.}$$

1.—*Oxide of Lead.* There are three oxides of lead, viz. the yellow, the red, and the brown: composed as follows,

Yellow oxide, ...Oxygen 7.7.
Lead 92.3.

Red.............Oxygen 11.55.
Lead 88.45.

Brown..........Oxygen 15.4.
Lead 84.6.

All the oxides of lead may be reduced to the metallic state, by heating them with a mixture of tallow and charcoal, which will absorb the oxygen.

2.—*Sulphate of Lead. Lead vitriol.* It consists of oxide of lead 71, sulphuric acid 25; with small proportions of water of crystallization and oxide of iron. Its colour is grey whitish. It dissolves in strong muriatic acid when the action of the solvent is promoted by heat. It is immediately reduced before the blow-pipe. It has been found in Velenoweth Mine, near St. Ives, Cornwall. Crystallized in rectangular octahedrons with obtuse pyramids and rhomboidal prisms:—and quadrangular prisms with a pyramid.

3.—*Muriate of Lead.* It consists of oxide of lead 85, carbonic acid 6, muriatic acid 8. The crystals are a cube frequently truncated. Its colour is straw yellow; sometimes, white, with a lustre far superior to that of carbonate of lead. It is a rare mineral.

4.—*Phosphate of Lead.* Its colour is brown or yellowish green. The *brown* consists of oxide of lead 78, phosphoric acid 18, with a small proportion of muriatic acid. It has been found in Huel Penrose, of a yellowish colour, crystallised in hexahedral prisms. The *green phosphate* consists of oxide of lead 76, phosphoric acid 13, arsenic acid 7, with small proportion of muriatic acid and water. Specimens of a yellowish green in minute dodecahedrons have been found in Huel GoldenMine, Perranzabuloe, and Huel Penrose, Helston. It is soluble in nitric acid, but does not effervesce. All the ores of lead are reducible to the metallic state before the blow-pipe, except phosphate, which becomes a whitish crystalline mass, covered with fine acicular crystals laid in all directions.

Sulphuro-phosphate of Lead. Blue Lead. In the end of summer, 1822, a variety of lead-ore was found on the back of the lode of Huel Hope, Perranzabuloe, different from any hitherto known in Cornwall. The specimens were bought up with avidity. The specimens are of the colour of lead, exposed to the weather, crystallized in six-sided prisms of various lengths and thickness, obliquely diverging from a common centre: terminated by hexahedral pyramids, and truncated, which are the most rare:—opaque, heavy. Some of the crystals are about two inches long, others are small and fascicular: Several of the groups

have the crystals bending with their heads
downwards, and give an idea of a weeping
willow. When the specimen is broken, the
interior presents a scopiform crystallization,
promiscuously aggregated. They are brittle,
the fracture smooth and shining. From their
lead colour they are very conspicuous in collections. A piece was placed by Mr. Michell
before the blow-pipe on charcoal; it emitted
sulphurous vapour, and, similar to phosphate
of lead, became crystallized in a light waxen
yellow enamel, on the surface of which were
laid in different directions very fine acicular
crystals, like those formed, when yellow
phosphate is melted, but not so numerous: it
was therefore agreed that the specimen consists of lead, sulphur, and a small portion of
phosphoric acid, and it is named *sulphuro-
phosphate of Lead.* At the time of writing
(March, 1825,) a fresh *bunch* of this ore has
been found in Huel Hope; the form of the
crystals is the same as the above, only with
this difference, they are all studded with brilliant minute hexadrons.

5.—*Carbonate of Lead. White Lead-Ore.*
—Next to galena, it is the most generally diffused. It is sometimes yellow, or brown.
It consists of oxide of lead 82, carbonic acid
18. It dissolves with effervescense in muriatic and nitric acids. It occurs commonly
crystallized in six-sided prisms, terminated by six or four-sided summits. The
crystals are small. It is transparent and
translucent. It refracts double in a high degree. Decrepitates before the blow-pipe, and
is reduced to a globule of lead. It has been
found in Pentire Glaze, St. Minver; Huel
Penrose and Park Matthew's, St. Austell; and

Huel Golden, Perranzabuloe. *Black Lead Ore.* It consists of oxide of lead 79, carbonic acid 18, with a small proportion of carbon. Crystals six-sided prisms. The *Acicular Carbonate*, remarkably beautiful, has been found in Pentyre, near Padstow. It is snow-white. —It occurs also in Huel Alfred and Huel Ann.

6.—*Chromate of Lead.* It consists of oxide of lead 63, chromic acid 36. It is orange red, or yellow. Fusible *per se.* It decrepitates before the blow-pipe, and some lead is reduced. It does not effervesce with acids. It is crystallized in four-sided prisms. The beautiful pigment known in commerce by the name of chrome-yellow, or chromate of lead, is prepared from the basis of chromate of iron, and formed by saturating the chromate of potash with acetate of lead.

7.—*Arseniate of Lead.* It consists of oxide of lead 69, arsenic acid 26, with a small proportion of muriatic acid. It is yellow. Translucent. Before the blow-pipe it gives out arsencial vapours, and the strong odour distinguishes it. It occurs in hexahedral prisms, the lustre of which is resinous. Beautiful specimens have been found in the United Mines, and Huel Unity, which were capillary crystals and large six-sided prisms. It has also been found in Huel Gorland and North Downs, Mines; in the parish of Endellion and in Beeralstone lead mines, Devonshire. Specimens of this were analized by Mr. Gregor, from Huel Unity, in 1809, and the result was,

Oxide of lead......69.76
Arsenic acid........26.40
Muriatic acid...... 1.58
—————
97.74

Arseniate of lead and copper from Huel Alfred (1825.) Colour, when fresh broken, leek green. Mammillated, and in coarse granular concretions, with patches here and there of the arseniate of lead, of a greyish white colour. Before the blow-pipe on charcoal it emits arsenical fumes, and is reduced to globules of lead and copper: Mr. Michell found it to contain

Protoxide of lead....31.5
Peroxide of copper...28.0
Arsenic acid........24.0
Peroxide of iron...... 2.0
Silica.............10.0
Water............... 2.0

Arsenio-phosphate of lead. In the end of 1824, a new variety of crystallized lead-ore was found in the cross-lode of Huel Alfred, the crystals are splendent, of a rich topaz colour, the bases of the prisms smooth, they are hexahedrons; some have their terminal and lateral edges replaced; while in others, the hexagon is perfect; they are translucent; the groups are frequently found diverging from a common centre. Some of the crystals are nearly $\frac{1}{8}$ of an inch in length, and $\frac{2}{8}$ of an inch in diameter. In some of the crystalline recesses the minute crystals have been observed to have pyramids, and even some of the large. The specimens of this arsenio-phosphate of lead are very beautiful, and were bought up as soon as they made their appearance.[*]

[*] At the time of writing, many fine specimens of this mineral were in Mr. Tregoning's collection, at Truro. Mr. Tregoning has, for more than thirty years, been connected with the most intelligent working miners; and from his intimate acquaintance with the productive districts, he is put in possession of the best specimens from every new discovery of real interest, which never fail to draw the attention of collectors. His indefatigable industry and his acute discrimination have identified him with Cornish mineralogy, and have contributed to the advancement of practical science.

Molybdate of Lead. Yellow Lead-Ore.—It consists of oxide of lead 58, molybdic acid 38, with small proportions of oxide of iron and silica. It decrepitates and fuses before the blow-pipe into a grey mass, in which a globule of reduced lead is found. The crystals octahedrons. Its colour is a wax yellow. It is soluble in muriatic acid.

Sulphuret of Lead. Galena.—It consists of lead 85, sulphur 13, and a trace of iron. The primitive form of its crystals is a cube. It is not perfectly soluble in nitric acid. The acid, parting with some of its oxygen to the lead, produces nitrous gas, but the acid is only partly decomposed, as the sulphur is left behind. It is distinguished from *blende*, or *sulphuret of zinc*, by its lustre remaining when scratched with a knife, while that of zinc-ore is destroyed. Galena is abundant in Cornwall. It was found formerly in large cubes in Tresavean mine, with copper pyrites; at Poldice; and Penrose mine, in a rich vein that opened on the surface. Lately, in Garras mine, near Truro. At present, in Huel Rose mine, Newlyn. It generally contains silver. That of Huel Pool, yielded 60, and that of Garras 70 ounces of silver in the ton. (See *Silver*.)

Bournonite, Antimonial lead-ore.—Count Bournon first discovered it in Huel Boys, Parish of Endellion, Cornwall, and gave it the name of *Endellione* from the Parish, it is now called after his own name. It is intermediate between lead grey and steel grey. Crystals large four-sided rectangular prisms. Its constituent parts are lead 42, 62, antimony 24, 28, copper 12, 8, sulphur, 17, with a trace of iron. When thrown in powder on a hot iron, it emits a phosphorescent light of a bluish-white colour, but without smell. It splits and decrepitates before the blow-pipe; emits sulphureous vapours; colours the charcoal around of a clove-brown; after which there remains a crust of sulphureted lead, which is easily broken with the point of a knife, inclosing a bead of lead.

Earthy Lead-Ore.—Some years ago, Lord Falmouth, the owner, and having a part in the adventure, sent a specimen of this, from Huel Mexico, in Perranzabuloe, of which there was a considerable quantity, to Mr Michell, whose analysis follows. It appears to have suffered a partial decomposition; it occurs amorphous, and crystallized in very minute six sided prisms, lining the cavities of ferruginous quartz, and attaching to, and mixed with, fragments of hematitic-iron ore. Colour, straw-yellow, greenish, and yellowish grey, soluble in nitric acid, without effervescence. Before the blow-pipe on charcoal it melts into a black brilliant mass, and globules of the compound metals of lead and silver are speedily reduced, with the emission of a little vapour:

Composed of Lead..20.2
Iron...24.6
Silver.. 2.4
Silica.. 37
Oxigen 14

With a trace of chloric acid.

Uses of Lead.—Nearly all the lead of commerce is obtained from galena.

Lead immersed in water becomes covered with a white crust of oxide, or carbonate, which is a most destructive poison. River water is more liable to receive an impregnation from leaden vessels than spring water.

The use of earthenware glazed with oxide of lead is hazardous, as it is soon corroded by any acid liquor. Fermented liquors, prepared or kept in such vessels, have caused fatal accidents.

A small quantity of arsenic added to melted lead, disposes it to run into drops. Poured into a vessel with holes, the drops are congealed in water. Sifted on the end of an inclined plane, the spherical ones roll down; the pear-shaped waddle aside. The former are small shot. In London the furnace is at the top of a high tower; and the shot cools as it falls through the air. It is glazed by being tossed in a vessel with black lead.

The Chinese cast thin sheets of lead for tea chests, by letting the metal run through a horizontal slit at the bottom of a box, which is drawn along, and the sheet congeals behind.

Melted lead oxidizes rapidly: a wrinkled pellicle is renewed as soon as the former one is raked off; by this means the whole may be carried away. Grease on the surface prevents this oxidation. In furnaces, bellows blow slantingly on the middle of melted lead, and the oxide is driven without intermission to one side. The vapours of the oxide in this process are extremely injurious to health. When congealed, the oxide is yellow, of a plated texture, and is *Litharge ;* the lead gains about 1-10th in weight by oxidation. The oxide of all metals is encreased by its combination with air. By a strong continued heat litharge loses its yellow colour and burns orange, and bright red; this is *red lead,* or *minium.*

Loose rolled sheets of lead are set in a bed of tan over vinegar; the surface becomes covered, by the vapour of the acid, with white-

D

lead; which is scraped off at intervals, until
the whole is dissolved. This is the ceruse
used in painting. It is easily dissolved in
acetate acid, and affords a sweet salt, which is
sugar of lead—a deadly poison.

Dealers in wines occasionally sweeten them
when ascescent. Sulphuretted hydrogen water
will throw down any deleterious adulteration
of lead in a dark brown sulphuret. A good
dose of Epsom, or Glauber salt, counteracts the
effects of sugar of lead, by converting the acetate of lead into an innoxious sulphate. Earths
exposed to melting heats with the oxide of
lead melt, and form glassy compounds; hence,
it is employed in making flint glass, artificial gems, and enamels. Litharge boiled
in vinegar is *Goulard's Lotion;* cooling in
external inflammations, and all fiery eruptions
of the skin.

Oxide of lead becomes thick in oil, and is
the basis of plasters, paints, &c.

Yellow chromate of lead, ground with about
two-thirds, by weight, of tritoxide of lead, and
mixed with hot water, unite into a red sub-
chromate. This gives a permanent orange
scarlet upon cotton. Scarlet sub-chromate of
lead is very beautiful as a *paint*, when ground
with oil. It mingles with other colours; nor
is it changed by time.

White lead and linseed oil boiled, contract
a skin impenetrable by the air or weather.
Litharge fused with salt decomposes it; the
oxide unites with the muriatic acid, and forms
a yellow paint.

Tin melted with lead forms a compound
much more fusible than lead itself, and is
used as a solder for lead.

Two balls of lead, a small place being

Scraped where they are to come in contact, will,
with, a twist adhere; no other metal does this.
Fill a tumbler with water; place a piece of
white paper over it; invert it on the hand; the
paper will keep up the water; hang it from
the lower ball by a string passing through a
hole in its centre and they will afford a subject
for a philosophical conversation. If lead-ore
yield 75 lbs of metal out of 100 it is considered
rich, if only 40, it is not worth working.

VII. PALLADIUM.

Palladium occurs native in grains with a
metallic lustre, intermixed with *platinum* or
alloying it, and only distinguishable from it
by its greater hardness and gravity. It is
greyish white; and very malleable. Its fracture, fibrous, in diverging striæ, showing a
slight crystallized arrangement. It is reducible *per se*. If touched while hot with a bit
of sulphur, it flows like zinc; the sulphur is
dissipated and the malleable metal remains.
It forms a deep red solution with nitric acid.

VIII. RHODIUM.

Rhodium, like the former, is found among
the crude grains of platinum. With borax it
acquires a white metallic lustre, but remains
infusible. With sulphur and arsenic it readily
unites; and like palladium it acquires fusibility; but, on the expulsion of these alloys by
means of heat, the metal is not rendered malleable.

IX. SILVER.

Silver, besides being found *native* is com-
D 2

bined with the *muriatic, carbonic,* and *sulphuric,* acids; and alloyed with *sulphur, gold, antimony, arsenic, lead, copper, bismuth, alumina, and selenium, forming*

> *Muriate* }
> *Carbonate* } *of silver.*
> *Sulphuret* }
> *Auriferous silver.*
> *Antimonial silver.*
> *Bismuthic silver.*
> *Seleniuret of silver.*

Silver has almost no affinity with oxygen; hence, it is not found in nature in the state of an oxide; and when it is brought by chemical means to that state, its affinity to oxygen is so weak, that it can be destroyed by the mere application of heat.

1.—*Muriate of Silver, Kerate.*—It consists of silver 76, muriatic acid 16, oxigen 7, with small proportions of alumina and oxide of iron. It is the most beautiful and rich variety of silver ore. It is fusible in the flame of a candle;—transluscent;—amorphous;—occurs sometimes in cubes or parallelopipids. A variety of muriate, consists of silver 67.75, muriatic acid 21, sulphuric acid 0.25, oxide of iron 6, alumina 1.75, lime 0.25. Breathed on, and rubbed by a piece of iron or zinc, the surface exhibits a film of reduced silver. Heated by the blow-pipe with an alkali, it exhales an unpleasant odour, melts, and gives a globule of silver.

2.—*Carbonate of silver*—consists of silver 72, carbonic acid 12, oxide of antimony and a trace of copper 15. It effervesces in nitric acid. It is grey, or iron black. Infusible *per se.*

3.—*Antimonial silver-ore*—consists of silver 89, antimony 11. Its colour is generally silver-white, or tarnished yellow. It occurs massive. Before the blow-pipe the antimony flies off, and a bead of silver remains. Of this there are 1.—Red silver-ore—consisting of silver 60, antimony 19, sulphur 19, and a little oxygen. It occurs crystallized in an obtuse rhomboid. 2.—Arsenical silver-ore—consisting of arsenic 35, iron 44, silver 12, antimony 4. It is generally tarnished black.

4.—*Bismuthic Silver-Ore*—consists of bismuth 27, lead 33, silver 15, iron and sulphur 15. Its colour is a light lead grey.

5.—*Seleniuret*—consists of silver 33.33, copper 23.05, selenium 26, other substances 8.90. It is of a shining lead grey, with a granular texture; yields readily to the knife; leaving a silvery lustre. Before the blow-pipe, it emits an odour like horse-radish, and melts into a bead of grey metal.

6.—*Sulphuret of lead and silver* from one lodein Huel Rose, Newlyn parish, (in February, 1822) produced 77 per cent. of lead, which contained between 60 and 65 ounces of silver in the ton. Sulphuret from the south lode, on an average, made a produce in lead of 67 per cent, and 1000 parts of the metal contained 2.01 of silver=65 oz. 13 dwts. 4 grs. The ore from another lode produced, on an average, from the furnace, about 77 per cent. of lead, and the metal contained about 60 ounces in the ton.

The process of separating silver from lead is known by the name of *refining*. The lead is placed gradually on a dish called a test, made by beating a mixture of burnt bones and fern ashes into an iron hoop, giving the surface a concave form to a certain depth. Being acted on by the flame of the furnace, aided by a

D 3

current of air from a pair of bellows, it gradually assumes a kind of vitriform state, and is blown off the test, or sinks into it, while the silver remains unaltered. By this process the lead is converted into a substance called *litharge*, and which consists of fine scales partly of a red and partly of a golden yellow colour. It is compounded of yellow oxide of lead, combined with a certain portion of carbonic acid. Refined lead is this substance reduced again to a metallic state, but it still retains a portion of silver. Thus, 1000 parts of refined lead sent from the above mine, by Sir C. Hawkins, Bart. the proprietor, to the Royal Institution of Cornwall, contained 0.08 of silver, equal to 470 grains in the ton.

Silver in Cornwall is generally associated with galena (the sulphuret of lead). The following are the other mines of Cornwall, in which silver and its combinations have been found.

Huel Mexico, in Perranzabuloe, has produced native silver, with argentiferous galena; muriate of silver, massive and in cubes.

Herland Mine, in Gwinear, has produced native silver embedded in a soft marle; antimonial silver; sulphuret of silver, in cubes, and massive, in the cross lode.

Huel Alfred, in Phillack, has produced native silver in green carbonate of copper.

Huel Ann, in Phillack, has produced native capillary silver, with surprising fineness of fibre, in tin white and grey cobalt, and grey silver in arsenical pyrites.

Dolcoath, in Camborne, has produced native, and sulphuret of silver.

Huel Basset, in Illogan, has produced native silver, and sulphuret with galena.

Huel Duchy, near Callington, has produced native, grey, black, and red sulphuret of silver, and red antimonial sulphuret, in the cross lode, both massive and crystallized.

Huel St. Vincent, near Callington has produced native silver, with muriate, and sulphuret of silver.

Willsworthy Mine, on the borders of Devon, has produced native silver accompanied by yellow copper and arsenical cobalt.

Native silver has also been found in *St. Mewan* and *St. Stephens.*—Crinnis Mine, in the parish of St. Austle, has produced silver in conjunction with pyrites of copper and antimonial ore.

Silver is perfectly cleaned from the tarnish of sulphurous gas, by soot and vinegar.

Diluted nitric acid is the best solvent of silver. During the effervescence the metal is oxidated by attracting oxygen from a part of the acid, and forms nitrous air; the rest unites with the oxidated silver, and forms nitrate of silver. If the solution remain green, the silver has been tainted with copper.

When the element oxygen is not retained by a very strong affinity, light expels it from its combinations. Nitric acid exposed to the solar rays, loses its oxygen, and becomes yellow, and at length acquires a purple hue. Silver compounded with this acid grows black in the light. A piece of paper moistened with the solution, becomes blackened in a few minutes. To this action of light is owing the alteration of the shades of metallic paints. The solution diluted, stains wood, bones, marble, agate, and jasper, black; and in a weaker state, it stains hair, silk, cambric, and lawn, brown:—and is used as indelible ink for marking linen, and for taking copies of paintings on glass. The nitrate is reduced to hexahedral or octahedral crystals by evaporation. Deprived of their water of crystallization by fusion, they are moulded in cylindrical pieces called *lunar caustic*, and are used by surgeons to corrode fungous excrescences. It is a most powerful antiseptic. Meat impregnated with it doesnot putrify. On the application of common salt, this acid is expelled. The muriatic acid is the most strongly attracted by silver. It separates it from every other acid. If muriatic acid, or any compound containing it, be added to the solution of silver in nitric acid, the silver instantly quits its solvent, and joins the muriatic, subsiding in a coagulum nearly insoluble in water. This is the muriate of silver. By adding the nitrate, the most minute quantity of muriatic acid, or of common salt, is discovered in water, by its becoming milky.

Silver is recovered from its solution in nitric acid in an entertaining manner. Copper attracts from the silver both the acid and the oxygen. The silver crystallizes in a thick downy covering on the copper, which viewed through a microscope resembles the down of feathers, or the foliage of vegetables. Put some of the solution on a shallow concave plate of glass; drop a bit of copper in it, a silver fringe will immediately form all around, and its ramifications will extend till all the silver is precipitated.

A single drop of the diluted solution placed before the microscope, and a particle of copper made to touch its edge, a stem will arise immediately, branching by starts, and in a few

minutes the little brush will occupy the whole
field of view.

Leaf silver made red hot on glass, or porcelain, penetrates it, and tinges it of a deep
yellow colour. The smoky flame of burning
vegetables brings out the beautiful colour, seen
in various elegant enamels.

One-twelfth part of copper is the alloy for
standard silver: or from 11oz. 2dwts. of fine
silver, and 18dwts of copper to the pound, are
coined 62 shillings.

The dial plates of clocks, and the scales of
barometers are silvered, by rubbing upon them
a mixture of the muriate of silver, sea salt,
and tartar. The silver is precipitated from
the muriatic acid which unites with the cop-
pery surface.

A thin plate of silver applied to a bar of
copper, with a little borax between them, the
two bound together, are exposed to a red heat;
the borax melts, and the silver adheres to the
copper; the bar is passed through the rolling
press; and thus lengthened, comes out *plated*.
French plating is performed by applying
leaves of silver successively to heated copper,
and fixing them by burnishing.

Copper is *silvered* with a powder of between 15 and 20 grains of silver, precipitated
from nitric acid by copper, mixed with tartar
and common salt; each 2 drachms and half a
grain of alum: it is polished with leather.
Saddlers and harness-makers, for ordinary
uses, cover their wares with tin.

X. BISMUTH.

Bismuth, besides being found *native*, is combined with *oxygen*, and the *carbonic* acid, and mineralized by *sulphur*, forming

    Oxide
    Carbonate } of Bismuth.
    Sulphuret

1.—*Native Bismuth*, discovered 1641, occurs massive, and crystallized in cubes, octahedrons, tetrahedrons, and rhomboids. Its texture foliated. Its colour silver-white, verging to red. It is frequently tarnished, or variegated red, yellow, or purple. In its external appearance it resembles antimony; is nearly as brittle, and exhibits a similar texture when broken. But it is much heavier, and its best whiteness is tinged with red. It melts before the flame of a candle. It is volatilized before the blow-pipe in white vapour, which is deposited on the charcoal, and its oxide fuses with borax into a yellow glass.

It has been found in Trugoe mine, parish of St. Columb; united with arsenical cobalt in Huel Sparnon, near Redruth; and in Herland mine.

It has also occured in two of the tin and copper lodes of Botallack, St. Just, in coarse red jasper.

The presence of this metal is ascertained by the miners exposing the stones supposed to contain it to a dull red heat, when it quickly oozes out, and it remains on the surface like globules of quicksilver.

In the sulphuric acid, only when strong and heated, it becomes oxydated by attracting oxygen from the acid; but it does not dissolve. The nitric acid dissolves it with much effervescence, and great heat; red vapours of nitrous gas are extricated, as the metal abstracts oxygen from the acid.

2.—*Oxide of Bismuth.* It consists of oxide of bismuth 86, oxide of iron 5, with a small proportion of carbonic acid and water. It has no lustre, but an earthy texture. It is rare, and generally accompanied by cobalt-ore. It is easily volatilized by the blow-pipe and reduced to the metallic state on charcoal. It dissolves in acids with effervescence. It has been found at Roach, and St. Agnes.

3.—*Carbonate of Bismuth.* Mr. Gregor writes, (*Annals of Philosophy*, vol. 8,) " it was " given to me several years ago as a carbo- " nate of bismuth, by Mr. J. Michell:—*the* " *credit of the discovery, therefore, belongs to* " *him.*" Mr. Michell discovered it in Huel Coates, a little to the north-west of St. Agnes Beacon. It consists of carbonate of bismuth and a portion of oxide of bismuth, mixed with stony matter. It assumes various tints of greyish green, and brownish and yellowish grey. Small patches of quartz and stony matter are discoverable in it. It effervesces in nitric acid. Mr. Michell has found it also in the mine " Cost all Lost," in the parish of Roach. " It is said to have occurred at Tre- " gurthy and St. Columb." (*Phillips.*)

4.—*Sulphuret of Bismuth.* Its constituent parts are bismuth 60, sulphur 40. Its colour is light lead grey. The powder black. It soils. It is fusible in the flame of a candle. It emits a reddish yellow smoke, and a blue flame before the blow-pipe. It does not effervesce in acids. It has been found in Dolcoath mine, in minute crystals; at Botallack, in yellowish white crystals; and at Huel Sparnon, in tin white crystals. It has also occurred in Huel Cock, St. Just, in minute grey crystals, tarnished yellow internally, embedded in and internally mixed with vitreous copper-ore, (sulphuret of copper) It also occurs in a stream-work in the parish of St. Columb, of a dark lead grey colour, in the state of water worn pebbles.

Bismuth is perfectly soluble in solution of nitric acid. Affusion of water readily decomposes it; that liquid absorbing its acid, and leaving the white oxide of this metal combined with a small portion of acid. This subnitrate was formerly known by the name of *magistry of bismuth ;* and is used for painting the skin to which it imparts a beautiful white. The gas of mineral coal, or sulphuretted hydrogen gas, renders the paint black. This property is the cause of the phenomenon produced by applying a solution of alkaline sulphuret to a letter written with a solution of bismuth, called *sympathetic ink.*

If a small portion of muriatic acid be mixed with the nitric, and the precipitated oxide be washed in cold water, it appears in minute scales of a pearly lustre, and is the *pearl powder* of perfumers.

Bismuth readily unites in fusion with all metals except zinc and arsenic, rendering them fusible in a less degree of heat. One part of bismuth, 5 of lead, and 3 of tin form *plumbers' solder.*

Bismuth 8 parts, lead 5, tin 3, fuze at a heat no greater than 212 deg. The mixture may be fused in a piece of stiff paper over a candle. Spoons made of it melt as soon as they are put into hot water.

Tin by a small addition of bismuth becomes hard and sonorous *pewter.* With lead and tin combined with mercury it is used in *soils* for mirrors. It is also used in the composition of *printers' types*. The sub-salt of this metal is used for giving a black colour to the hair, and the metal for refining gold and silver.

Bismuth is used in the *adulteration* of quick-silver. Lead alone would cause a diminu-tion of its mobility. The addition of a little bismuth prevents this.

Equal parts of tin, bismuth, and mercury, (the tin and bismuth being first melted, and when becoming solid, the quicksilver being added,) form *Mosaic silver:* from its flakey silvery appearance, it is used to embellish plaster casts, paper, &c.

Bismuth flows the thinnest of all the metals, and expands in congealing, it there-fore takes the finest impression of its mould; and as it gradually acquires hardness, it is useful in *taking impressions* of medals.

XI. URANIUM.

Uranium consists of oxide of uranium 86, protoxide* of iron 2, galena 6, silica 5. It is velvet or greyish black; deep grey; soft; very brittle. It occurs in thick curved la-mellar, and in course anglo-granular concre-tions. It has been found in Tin Croft and Tolcarn mines, Gwennap. *Uranite;—uran-mica;—hydrate of Uranium.* It is green;

---

* A protoxide denotes the metal combined with the first dose, or minimum of oxygen, which the metal is capable of forming. Deut-oxide will denote the second oxide of a metal, or the metal com-bined with two doses of oxygen. When a metal has combined with as much oxygen as possible, (which is the case with tin stone) the compound is then known by the term peroxide, indicating by it that the metal is thoroughly saturated with oxygen. We have therefore the term of oxide to denote the combination of metals with oxygen, in general; the terms protoxide and peroxide to denote the mini-mum and maximum of oxidation; and the terms deutoxide and tritoxide, &c. to denote all the intermediate states which are capable of being formed.

yellow; translucent; dissolves in nitric acid and gives it a lemon yellow colour.· Its constituent parts are oxide of uranium 74, oxide of copper 8, water 15. It occurs in thin leaves; or crystallized in rectangular four-sided tables; cubes, or octahedrons. It has been found in Carharrack, Tin Croft, Tolcarn, Huel Unity, and Huel Gorland;—Stenna Gwyn, St. Stephens, and Gunnis Lake mine, near Callington.

It occurs crystallized in quadrangular tables of which the angles are sometimes truncated, in four-sided prisms, with the lateral, and occasionally the terminal edges, replaced; in needle-form aud spear-form crystals, forming druses and botryoidal and globular concretions, in Huel Edward, St. Just. Its colour varies from white through various shades of green and rusty brown. In some instances, the extremities of the crystals have appeared nearly black. The needle-form crystals have occurred white; yellowish-white; bright-yellow; and the same crystal has sometimes been found partly green, and partly yellow. Uranite, from Gunnis Lake mine, is a phosphate of uranium, consisting of oxide of uranium 60, oxide of copper 9, phosphoric acid 15.3, water 13.8, and a trace of silex. Uranite of an emerald green, occurs (1825) in cubes and parallelograms in Huel Buller, Redruth. Before the blow-pipe with borax it gives a yellowish-green glass. It combines with vitriable substances, and gives them a brown or green colour:—on porcelain, with the usual flux, it produces an orange-yellow colour.

Mr. Gregor, in 1805, found in uranite, besides oxide of uranium, lime, oxide of lead,

and silica:—and in 1815, from a green variety, he separated 74, 4 per cent. of oxide of
uranium, containing a trace of oxide of lead,
8, 3 of oxide of copper, and 15, 4 of water.
Berzelius, in 1819, found, that the uranite of
Cornwall, before the blow-pipe, gave off an
odour of arsenic, and that the globule of copper, obtained with the assistance of soda, was
white and brittle; hence, he concluded, that
the gresn colour is occasioned by the presence
of arseniate of copper. He has subsequently
found, that the uranite of Cornwall consists of

Oxide of copper 8.44
Oxide of uranium 60.25
Phosphoric acid with }
arsenic acid . . . .} 15.56
Water 11.05
Gangue 0.70
           ———
           100.

From these analyses uranite is considered
a donble subphosphate of the oxide of uranium; the one with the oxide of copper, the
other with lime. And, as lime and oxide of
copper are isomorphous, they must, when
combined with an equal number of atoms of
oxide of uranium, phosphoric acid and water,
assume the same crystalline form, the two
minerals are, therefore, with respect to crystallization, identical; while their composition
shews them to to be of different mineralogical
species. The green uranite of Cornwall has
been called *chalcolite* : while the yellow variety retains the name of *uranite.*

———

XII. COPPER.

Copper besides being found *native* is combined with *oxygen*, the *sulphuric*, *muriatic*, *phosphoric*, *carbonic*, and *arsenic* acids, and mineralized by *sulphur*, and *silica*, forming

> *Oxide*
> *Sulphate*
> *Muriate*
> *Phosphate* ⎫
> *Carbonate* ⎬ *of copper.* *
> *Arseniate*
> *Sulphuret*
> *Silicate*

1.—*Native*, or *malleable copper*, consists of copper 99, with a trace of iron. Of its various crystallization, the cube is allowed to be the primary form; next to that the octohedron. It occurs also dendritic, capillary, massive, and in plates. Its colour, internally, is similar to that of purified copper. Copper beginning to be oxidated is coated with a reddish brown; a little more oxygen renders it blue; and the perfect oxide is a bright green, in which native copper is frequently found. Specimens are preserved like a dark purple mass of petrified moss. Considerable quantities have been raised near the Lizard, among which were massive pieces, having an incrustation of precious serpentine, very much resembling the green oxide of copper. A rare variety called thunderbolt copper, from its forked appearance, has been found in Huel Cock, St. Just. Tolvean, near Huel Cock, has produced a variety, consisting of fine wires, twisted like fillagree work. Arborescent native copper occurs also in Botallack mine.

---

* As the technical word *Vibgyor* enables us to remember the seven original colours of light, viz. violet, indigo, blue, green, yellow, orange, and red, so may *Noscamps* assist the memory in recollecting the different states of copper; each of the eight letters being the beginning of a name.

Huel Gorland, in Gwennap, has produced native copper in cubes and octahedrons. Huel Virgin near St. Day has produced it in cubes. Huel Music, and the United mines, have produced it crystallized. Huel Vor, near Helston, and Treskerby, near Redruth, have produced it in minute crystals, aggregated in a leaf-like form. Huel Prosper and Owan Vean, St. Hillary, and the Consolidated Mines, in Gwennap, have produced it in capillary crystals.

2.—*Oxide of copper*. *Red oxide*.—It consists of copper 87, 5, oxygen 12, 5. It is distinguished from red silver by its effervescence in nitric acid, and by splendent crystals, resembling a pea cut into octahedrons. It is sometimes crimson-red. It is translucent, and yields easily to the knife. Before the blow-pipe it is easily reduced *per se* on charcoal. It does not effervesce in muriatic acid. Its effervescence in the nitric is caused by the decomposition of the acid, by which a quantity of nitric acid gas is set at liberty. The gas thus separated when combined with the necessary proportion of oxygen forms nitric acid, and if the oxygen be separated from nitric acid, it assumes the form of this gas.

And, as metals are strongly disposed to combine with oxygen, they readily decompose substances to saturate themselves. But they will not unite with acids, unless previously oxidated:—and although red copper is a natural combination with oxygen, it is not combined with it to saturation. It therefore decomposes the nitric acid, as that acid contains oxygen very weakly united, and for this reason it is more easily separated from metals by heat, &c., the copper therefore disengages a quan-

E

tity of nitric acid gas, which, by its escape, occasions the effervescence. Muriatic acid is not liable to a similar decomposition, because its ingredients are more firmly united, and so strongly retained, that it cannot be separated by heat, but volatilizes the metal along with itself, and as the ore contains a sufficient proportion of oxygen to render it soluble in that acid, red copper is dissolved in it without effervescence.

The acids act on metals in proportion to the quantity of oxygen they have to impart. The nitric is the most effectual in oxidizing metals; next the sulphuric. The muriatic is more slow; but if the metal be slightly oxidated by heat or nitric acid, no acid unites with it more strongly

Red-oxide of copper has been abundantly found crystallized and massive in Huel Gorland, Huel Muttrel, and Huel Unity, Gwennap, —three mines on the same lode. Botallack has produced it in capillary crystals and in minute cubes and octahedrons. It has occurred crystallized in Huel Speed and Carvath, near St. Ives; in Huel Music, St. Agnes; West Huel Virgin; Carharrack in Gwennap; in Tincroft near Redruth; in Polgine and Huel Prosper; and in Gunnis Lake Mine, on the banks of the Tamar.

Tile-ore, or *Ferruginous red-copper*. The red varieties of Tile-ore contain the greatest quantity of copper; and the brown, the greatest quantity of iron. It yields to the knife, and sometimes to the nail. It is composed of red-oxide of copper and iron. It is frequently found incrusting quartz crystals. It occurs massive in Huel Edward, St. Just.

The *Black oxide*, composed of oxide of cop-

per and oxide of iron, of a brownish-black
colour, has been found in Huel Edward.

3.—*Sulphate of copper*—consists of oxide
of copper 32.13, sulphuric acid 31.57, water
30.13. It is called "Blue Vitriol." It is blue,
or bluish green. It is found stalactitically crystallized. The crystals are generally a cuneiform octahedron, in which state and also
fibrous, it has been found in Gunnis Lake
Mine, on the Tamar. A polished bar of iron
immersed in a solution of it, precipitates the
copper in its metallic state on its surface, from
the sulphuric acid having a greater affinity for
iron than for copper.

4.—*Muriate of copper*. It is also called *Ata-
camite*, because first discovered in the river
Lipas, in the desert of Atacama, which separates Chili from Peru. It occurs in minute
octahedral crystals, and in the form of green
sand. It consists of oxide of copper 73, muriatic acid 10, water 16. It dissolves in nitric
and muriatic acid without effervescence, and
exhales muriatic acid when heated with the
sulphuric. It has not been found in Cornwall.

5.—*Phosphate of copper*—consists of oxide
of copper 68, phosphoric acid 30. It is emerald green, but shaded and striated with blackish green, and to this colour the external natural surface approaches. It is opaque and
massive; and has a diverging striated texture,
and silky lustre. It does not assume a crystalline form, but the surface of some specimens
has a tendency to crystallization, namely, a
cuneiform octahedron. Its powder is verde-
gris green. It has been found in Gunnis Lake
Mine, on the Tamar. This mineral has been
mistaken for malachite, from its external resemblance.

E 2

6.—*Carbonate of copper*—is oxide of copper combined with carbonic acid, and forms two species, viz. the *blue* and the *green* carbonate. The latter is called malachite.

The blue carbonate consists of copper 66, carbonic acid 18, with small proportions of oxygen and water. It is crystallized in rhomboidal prisms, with four sided pyramids. Transluscent, frequently in the most complex crystals. The crystallized varieties of blue carbonate are of a deep uniform smalt-blue. The earthy varieties are pale, from a mixture of other substances, and are called " mountain blue," infusible *per se ;* with borax on charcoal it effervesces, gives a metallic bead, and colours the flux, green. It effervesces in nitric acid. The deep blue carbonate has been found in Tingtang mine, Gwennap, in granite. It has been found in small round spots in Huel Cock, St. Just; and in Huel Virgin, Carharrack, Huel Muttrel, Huel Gorland, and Huel Unity.

Malachite. This green carbonate consists of peroxide of copper 72, carbonic acid 18, water 9, and, it is said, of a small proportion of the basis of pure air. The cause of difference between blue and green carbonate is, that in the green the copper is combined with a greater proportion of oxygen, and more water than in the blue. Malachite seems to be formed from a gradual deposition of water containing oxide of copper, in the manner stalactitical calcareous spar is formed. It comprises two varieties, viz. 1—*mountain green,* which is massive, but it more frequently occurs in incrustation. It effervesces feebly with acids, and appears to consist of oxide and carbonate of copper with alumina and lime; 2.—

Malachite properly so called, which occurs massive and crystallized. It effervesces with acids. This effervescence in nitric acid distinguishes it from muriate and arseniate of copper.

Malachite has been found in Huel Husband, Huel Carpenter, in Huel Muttrel, Huel Unity, and Huel Gorland; it occurs in Huel Edward, St. Just, botryodal and incrustating quartz; and of various shades of green, yellow, brown, and black, accompanying arragonite, and also in Prince George Mine, Gwinear.

Anhydrous carbonate of copper consists of carbonic acid 16, peroxide of copper 60, peroxide of iron 19, with a small proportion of silver. It is brown, and is sometimes called *brown copper-ore.* It dissolves in acids, letting fall a red powder. It is often traversed by small veins of malachite.

7.—*Arseniate of copper* was first discovered in Cornwall about forty years ago, in Carharrack Mine, and afterwards in Tincroft. It consists of the following varieties,

1, *Octahedral arseniate:*—sky blue; verdigris green; translucent on the edges; fusible *per se :* with borax it affords a bead of copper: it consists of oxide of copper 49, arsenic acid 14, water 35. It has been found in the Gwennap Mines.

2. *Hexahedral arseniate:*—emerald green: it consists of copper 39, arsenic acid 43, and water. It fuses with borax and gives a bead of copper: found with the preceding variety; and in Gunnis Lake Mine, on the Tamar.

3. *Trihedral arseniate:*—deep celandine green; but owing to its ready oxidation, becomes tarnished with black, of which colour

E 3

some of its larger crystals, and its curved lamellar concretions appear outwardly; within they are blue; the minute crystals are a beautiful bluish-green. It consists of oxide of copper 54, arsenic acid 30, and water 16. It has been found in the Gwennap Mines.

4. *Prismatic arseniate* of copper:—olive-green; It consists of oxide of copper 60, arsenic acid 39.

5. *Hæmatitic arseniate* of copper; *wood-copper:*—brown; green; yellow:—the structure generally of a silky lustre; the small fibrous crystals of which it is composed are seen terminating over its surface. It consists of oxide of copper 50, arsenic acid 29, and water.

6. *Martial arseniate* of copper; *cupreous arseniate of iron:*—pale sky blue: sometimes tinged with green. It occurs in minute translucent prismatic crystals, with four sided pyramids. It consists of oxide of copper 22, arsenic acid 33, oxide of iron 27, with some silica.—A triple salt composed of the arsenic acid combined with the oxide of iron and of copper has been found in Carharrack Mine, Gwennap.

7. *Amianthiform arseniate* of copper:—green in various shades; yellow; white. It occurs in fine diverging flexible fibres, with a silky lustre. It consists of oxide of copper 50, arsenic acid 29, water 21. If the water of crystallization be evaporated, the fibres are dull. Fine specimens have been found in Tincroft Mine.

Prismatic arseniate, hæmatitic arseniate, martial arseniate, have been found in Cornwall only, in the Gwennap Mines. At the time of writing, (April, 1826,) beautiful specimens of arseniate of copper, of a milk-white colour, plumose, acicular, and radiated, are found in Tingtang Mine:—varieties of arseniate are also found in Pednandrae, Redruth.

8.—*Sulphuret of copper*, or *copper pyrites.—Yellow sulphuret of copper* is found in solid masses of an indeterminate shape; frequently crystallized in simple three sided pyramids; in double four sided pyramids; in six sided plates; in tetrahedrons, small, distinct, and of high polish; in octahedrons and dodecahedrons. When broken, it generally exhibits a conchoidal texture. Copper pyrites and grey copper are the only species of minerals, in which the regular tetrahedron is found. Iron pyrites never occur in tetrahedrons; but, professor Mohs says, the primary form of copper pyrites is an octahedron with a square base. It is the most abundant ore of the Cornish Mines. To give its localities would be to give the names of almost all the mines. It occurs in all classes of rocks in Cornwall, the greatest known depository of copper-ores. It yields to the knife, by which it is distinguished from iron-pyrites, which it often resembles, but which resists both the file and the knife. A specimen raised at Huel Towan, St. Agnes, was analyzed by Mr. Michell, and produced

Copper . . 30.0
Iron. 31.0
Sulphur . . 33.0
Silica . . . 3.0
Loss 3.0
———
100.

Sulphuret of copper of a dark purple has recently been found completely incrustating thick quartz crystals, both in plates and botryoidal. Sulphuret of copper (1825) in beautiful purple hexagonal plates coated with brilliant hexagonal prisms has been found in Huel Levant, in St. Just.

Copper pyrites from exposure to the air passes through numerous irridescent shades, principally purple, blue, and red. These become tarnished, and, at last, blended into a greenish brown. This colour is only superficial. The interior is uniformly yellow. It is the ore from which the great proportion of the copper of commerce is obtained. Copper predominates in the soft; iron, in the hard pyrites. To know if pyrites contain copper: pulverize and ustulate a small quantity, so that the sulphur may be evaporated: apply liquid ammonia to the remainder, and, if there be copper in it, a dark blue solution will be produced.

Variegated copper-ore;—*peacock-ore*;—*purple copper*:—it consists of copper 69, sulphur 19, with small proportions of iron and oxygen: its crystals are the cube and octahedron: it yields from 50 to 70 per cent. of copper. Its variegated colour seems to be owing to its having parted with some of its sulphur. The copper is slightly oxidated to which the variegated colour is owing. The beginning of oxidation of steel is indicated by a similar diversity of colours on its surface, as the oxygen of the atmosphere cannot penetrate farther; but in variegated copper the oxidating principle pervades the whole mass. And when a specimen is broken, from the metal being disposed to absorb more, the fresh surface by the oxygen of the air becomes brown. Purple copper occurs in Botallack, St. Just; Huel Jewell near St. Day; and Poldory, Cook's

Kitchen, Tincroft, and Dolcoath, near Redruth; and in Camborn Vean.

Grey copper;—Fahlerz. This species adds to the number of curious minerals for which Cornwall is so eminently distinguished. It occurs massive and in tetrahedrons. A specimen from Crinnis Mine St. Austle, analyzed by Mr. Michell gave the following,

Copper....46
Antimony..21
Iron.......17.2
Sulphur....14
Silver...... 1.8

It does not contain arsenic. This ore consisting of different minerals, renders analysis uncertain. Some specimens contain lead, while others possess a large proportion of silver.

Grey sulphuret of copper is common in Botallack, Levant, and Huel Spearn, St. Just. In the former mine, specimens have been found crystallized in octahedrons, and hexahedral plates crossing at right angles. In Levant, in crystals of six-sided prisms terminated by four-sided pyramids; and three-sided prisms terminated by three-sided pyramids. In Huel Spearn, crystallized in cubes.

Black Copper-Ore—consists of copper 37, antimony 22, sulphur 28, with small proportions of iron, and accidentally silver, lead, zinc and mercury. Its colour is iron black. It contains no arsenic. The crystals are tetrahedrons and sometimes hexahedrons.

White Copper-Ore;—arsenical copper pyrites;—the rarest species of copper-ore;—it consists of copper 40, with arsenic, iron and sulphur. It has been found with yellow pyrites in Huel Gorland, Gwennap.

9.—*Silicate of Copper ;—chrysocolla—*consists of copper 40, oxygen 10, silica 26, carbonic acid 7, water 17. It is verdigris green, and brownish red. It has been found massive, stalactitic, in Huel Unity, Huel Gorland, Huel Muttrel, and Carharrack, Gwennap, and Prince George, in Gwinear. It fuses with borax.

Emerald Copper ;—dioptase, is emerald green. It consists of oxide of copper 55, silica 33, water 12. It is translucent; the structure lamellar ; crystallized in six-sided prisms, terminated by three-sided pyramids. It has not been found in Cornwall.

To know if an ore contain copper, drop a little nitric acid on it ; then dip a feather into the acid, and wipe it over the blade of a knife ; if there be any copper it will be precipitated on the knife.

———

The sprinklings of copper which frequently occurred in the tin mines were considered as a species of yellow marcasite, or mundic, and it was called " poder." This uniting intimately with the tin on fusion debased its value, and its predominance in deep mines was one of the ordinary causes of their being discontinued ; as the extraction of the volatile matter by heat, it is presumed, was not known. The interest of those who first discovered this mineral so disagreeable to the tinner, to be copper-ore, made it for some time be kept a profound secret, so that the precise time is not ascertained. But it is believed to have been about the beginning of the last century. The

first discoverers formed themselves into a
company, and it is to them that the county
owes the present mode of *Ticketing* for copper-ores.

The copper-ore, on being raised from the
mines, is pounded and put into heaps of several tons. One is well mixed, and any sampler on an appointed day fixes on a third or
fourth of the dole. After subdividing, and
mixing this, &c. a sufficient quantity is put
into a bag by each sampler, and this is the
sample of the whole. These are carried to
the different Assay-Offices. Then the ore is
pulverized, and an ounce Troy is weighed. It
is assayed in a crucible with proper fluxes,
and after repeated operations a bead of copper
is found among the scoria. Now, if one ounce
Troy, of ore, make one pennyweight of copper, it will be 1 in 20. Five pennyweights
will be 5 in 20, &c. Therefore the metal in a
ton of ore may be known by asking how many
parts in 100 such a sample produced.

The *Standard* of copper is that price per ton
which it has been sold for in the market, and is
a term given by the smelter to denote a ton of
metal in the ore, from which (standard) he de-
ducts £2. 15s. for every ton of ore, or as many
as may be required according to its produce
to give a ton of copper, and which sum is considered by the smelter as an equivalent for
the returning charge, or the expence of reducing the ore to a merchantable state. The
produce is the proportion of metal obtained
on being assayed by fire which the ore contains, divided into one hundred parts, and
fractions of a part as low as one-eighth.
Hence, suppose a parcel of ore on being assayed makes $8\frac{1}{8}$th per cwt. at the standard of

120, i. e. the price which the purchaser can obtain for a ton of metal.

$$120$$
$$8\tfrac{1}{8} \text{ produce}$$

$$\tfrac{1}{8}\ 960$$
$$15$$

1,00) 9,75(£9. 15s.
20 £2. 15s. returning charge

15,00 £7. 0s. value of the ore per ton.

Every 20 shillings the standard rises or falls, will make a difference in the assay of 1 shilling; or a 20th in every pennyweight, and a halfpenny in every grain; as, for instance, one pennyweight one grain at £95 the standard, will make the produce equal to £4. 15s. the pennyweight, and three shillings and eleven pence half-penny the grain; but if the standard be 96, the produce will be valued at £4. 16s. the pennyweight, and four shillings the grain, deducting for returning charge.

A fortnight's interval takes place between the assay and the ticketing, during which time the agents receive answers from their principals, as to the price. Before dinner,* tickets containing offers from the different copper-companies founded on these assays are pro-

* When Boulton and Watt's patent steam-engines were erected in Cornwall, the produce of the French vintage was obtained at an easy rate;—so much so, that at the mine-dinners,—and probably from the wells being disturbed by the deep workings,—water was generally drank, mixed with a little wine, &c. Mr. Watt and his friend Dr. Robinson, soon after the engines were established, were entertained with a large company, at Camborne. Dr. Robinson called for a glass of water;—the servant, approaching respectfully, asked,—" did you say *clean* water, sir?" Turning round his manly countenance, not knowing the import of her words, " Lass!" replied the Professor of Natural Philosophy from the University of Edinburgh,—" Lass, dost thou think I drink *foul* water!"

duced, and the highest is the purchaser. The first copper-ores were carried to Bristol, " either to save cost in the fuel, or to conceal " the profit." Infant attempts to smelt the ore in the county were made at Polrudden, in St. Austle, in Phillack, in 1714; and in St. Agnes, " where copper was smelted with good " success:" and about the year 1754, Hayle works were erected.

Copper ores contain sulphur, iron, and arsenic. The sulphur and arsenic are gradually dissipated in the furnaces. The iron is vitrified with the matter intermixed with the ore, especially if it be quartz. This silicious stone greatly facilitates the extraction of the copper, as it has a strong disposition to unite with the calcined iron, and be converted with it into scoria; and thus, the iron is actually destroyed as a metal. The iron-ore is disregarded by the miner. The sulphur unites strongly with the copper, and increases its fusibility, and while they are uniting, a quantity of heat is extricated, which produces a sudden and bright ignition, and it makes the copper more readily subside from the scoria. Though the heat be not sufficient to melt the metal, but only the sulphur, if the metal be divided into small pieces, the sulphur penetrates it, and entirely changes its appearance.

Hayle copper works ceased a few years ago, and all the copper-ore of Cornwall is now sent to Wales, and we give an account of the mode of smelting it at the *Hafod Works*, abridged from Mr. VIVIAN's paper;—*Annals of Philosophy*, Feb. 1823.

1. Process. Copper-ore *calcined*. The heat as great as the ore will bear without being fused, or baked together. When sufficiently

cool to be removed, water is thrown over it to prevent the escape of the finer particles. It is *black* and *powdery*.

2. Process. Calcined ore *melted*. When the ore is melted, the earthy matter and metallic oxides, being specifically lighter, float on the surface and are skimmed off. The metal is made to flow into a pit of water. It then becomes *granulated;* and is called *coarse metal.* If the slags contain any copper, on being broken, it is found at the bottom. The oxide of iron gives them a black colour. The silex or quartz remains in part unfused and gives the slags a porphyritic appearance. The granulated metal contains about ⅓ of copper; composed chiefly of copper, iron and sulphur.

3. Process. *Calcination* of coarse metal. Similar to the calcining of the ore.

4. Process. *Melting* of the course metal after calcination. With the calcined metal are melted some slags, from the last operation which contain some oxide of copper, which becomes reduced by a portion of the sulphur which combines with the oxygen, and passes off as sulphurous acid gas, while the reduced metal combines with the sulphuret. The slags, being composed chiefly of the black oxide of iron, fuse readily, and act as solvents for earthy matter, &c. The metal after the slag is skimmed off is either tapped into water, or into sand-beds. In the granulated state, it is called *fine metal;* in the solid form, *blue metal,* from the colour of its surface.

5. Process. *Calcination* of the fine metal similar to that of the course metal.

6. Process. *Melting* of the calcined fine metal is similar to that of the coarse metal;

the product is a coarse copper containing from 80 to 90 per cent. of pure metal.

7. Process. *Roasting.* This is chiefly oxidizing. The pigs of coarse copper from the last process are exposed to the action of the air which draws through the furnace at a great heat. The volatile substances are expelled and the iron or other metals which remain, oxidized. The pigs are covered with black blisters, and the copper is called *blistered copper.* It is porous, honey-combed—from the gas formed during the ebullition which takes place in the sand-beds on tapping. It is nearly freed from all the sulphur, iron and other substances, with which it was combined.

8. Process.—An assay is taken out with a small ladle, and broken in a vice. The copper in this state is termed *dry.* Brittle, of a deep red, inclining to purple, an open grain and crystalline structure. In the process of toughening, the surface of the metal in the furnace is first well covered with charcoal. A pole commonly of birch, is then held in the liquid metal, which causes considerable ebullition, owing to the evolution of gaseous matter ; and this operation of *poling* is continued, adding occasionally fresh charcoal, that the surface may be covered until the refiner perceives, by repeated assays, the grain perfectly closed, and so as to assume a silky polished appearance when half cut through and broken, and is become of a light red colour. If it is soft under the hammer, and does not crack at the edges, he is satisfied of its *malleability.*

Copper for brass is granulated. With warm water the copper assumes a round form, and is called *bean shot.* With cold water it has a light ragged appearance, and is called *fea-thered shot*. The former is the state in which it is prepared for brass-wire making.

It is cast, for exports to the East Indies, in pieces 6 inches long, and weighing about 8 ounces, called *Japan copper*. These are dropped from the moulds, immediately on becoming solid, into cold water, and by a slight oxidation, the copper acquires a rich red colour on the surface.

A series of these results is preserved in the Royal Institution of Cornwall.

Uses of Copper.—100 parts of copper and about 10 of tin melted together are the composition of *cannon*. One part of copper and from four to ten of tin, compose *Bell-metal*;—for repeating watches zinc is added. To melting copper ½ of old copper is added, and to each hundred of the mixture, lead and tin, in equal parts, make *Roman bronze*.

Speculums of reflecting telescopes are composed of 32 parts of the best copper, 4 parts of brass, 16½ of tin, and 1¼ of arsenic. Copper and arsenic form the brittle compound *tombac,* which is sometimes called *white copper*.

Copper is granulated through a plate of iron perforated with small holes; calamine is pounded, calcined, and mixed with the divided copper and charcoal; these being exposed to a wind furnace, the zinc rises in vapour and combines with the copper, and this becomes *brass*.

Dutch Gold is hammered out from a mixture of copper and the purest calamine into leaves five-times thicker than gold-leaf.

Copper is employed in sheathing the bottom of ships. Strong solutions of salt, as brine, from their containing little, or no atmospheric air, the oxygen being excluded, do not affect copper; weak ones act strongly upon it. Bars of cast iron, three inches broad, and one inch thick, covering about 100th part of the surface of the copper, on each side of the keel from the stem to the stern, and fastened with copper spike-nails, on vessels, have produced a red crust, which was soft, to the depth of nearly half an inch. Scraped off, it had all the appearance of black lead; it soiled the fingers, and became hot, in a minute or two.

Copper vessels for *culinary* purposes are first scoured, then rubbed with sal-amoniac; they are then heated and sprinkled with powdered rosin, which prevents any slight film of oxide that would prevent the adhesion of the tin with which they are to be covered. It is then poured in and spread. Unctuous oils easily dissolve copper, or rust of copper; hence the dangerous effects produced by copper vessels used in cooking. Syrups and pickles may be hastily boiled in clean copper-vessels without being tainted, because the acid has not time to form an oxide. But a green or blue rust is very soon formed in a highly oxidated state, very dangerous, and very soluble in vegetable acids. Some cooks pour water which has stood in a cup over potash, to preserve the fresh green of peas, &c. Some, reckless of the consequences, it is said, have dared to put a copper piece among the boiling vegetables to produce the same effect!

Copper is used in *coinage*, either pure, or combined with gold and silver to increase their tenacity. Its oxide is used in colouring *glass* and *porcelain*, green.

When combined with acetic acid it forms

F

verdigris, which readily dissolves in distilled
vinegar. Evaporated, it gives crystals of a
dark-green. Pulverised, they constitute a
bright and elegant paint.

Copper does not strike fire with flint; and
though a rag be struck off red hot, it does not
kindle other inflammable bodies; hence, the
nails, hammers, hoops, and chisels, in powder
mills, are all of copper.

It is considerably softer when red hot. In
this state it was frequently coined in haste in
the Roman camp, with the general's die.
Compact malachite is used as a *green paint;*
and, as it takes a beautiful polish, is used on
jewellery.

Copper is artificially varnished, by polishing it, and then daubing its surface with the
deep red oxide of iron, called colcothar, (distilled from sulphate of iron,) or Spanish brown,
diluted with water, after which the copper is
heated, and the colcothar rubbed off. This
resists the weather.

Copper has such a capacity for heat, that
when melted it communicates it so rapidly
and so immensely to water, that the humidity
is instantaneously converted into highly elastic vapour, that, in founderies, the moulds are
heated red hot before any large work is cast in
them, else dreadful explosions might ensue.

Strong hot sulphuric-acid dissolves copper.
The metal attracts a portion of the oxygen of
the acid, and combined with the rest, becomes
white, which when dissolved in water, gives a
fine blue colour; from this by evaporation,
deep blue crystals of *blue vitriol* are obtained;
this is used in linen and cotton-printing. Crystals of nitrate of copper when bruised and
slightly moistened, and quickly wrapped in

tin-foil send out fumes; the mass becomes hot and brandishes forth desultory darts of flame and melted tin.

Lime water precipitates copper from some of its solutions. This oxide of the metal combined with a small quantity of lime or chalk is *verditer*,—a pleasant light blue.

Copper with equal parts of zinc forms *Bath-metal*, or similor. It has a rich yellow colour, and is formed into all sorts of goods, at Birmingham, by stamping and coining.

☞ The preceding article on copper had scarcely been printed, when there were laid before the author fine specimens of *Arseniate of Copper*, from Carharrack, Gwennap, of a mamillated form, covering, and here and there, filling up the interstices, or intermediate vacancies of rock crystals: the coating of a pale-green colour, which, in descending the section of the crystal towards the matrix, passes, by imperceptible gradations, into a perfect milk-white; has a rich silky lustre; compact; fibrous; radiated; and, in appearance, it much resembles the radiated character of wood-tin:——and specimens of

Red oxide of copper, occurs in Huel Charlotte, St. Agnes—mixed with native copper in globular massive groupes. The oxide of a deep crimson-colour, emitting, at a short distance, a glow superior to the richest velvet, crystallized in octahedrons, and delicate capillary prisms; transparent; and of high metallic splendor.

XIII. CADMIUM.

Cadmium has been discovered in the carbonate (calamine) and siliciform oxide of zinc.

F 2

Its colour is a fine white, slightly shaded with bluish-grey, much resembling tin in lustre, susceptibility of polish, and in crackling when bent, like tin, it stains paper, or the fingers, but is harder. It melts and crystallizes in octahedrons, presenting on its surface, as it cools, the appearance of fern-leaves. It is volatilised under a red heat. Its vapour, without smell, may be condensed like drops of quicksilver; and when congealing, they present traces of crystallization. It gives a transparent colourless glass-bead with borax. Nitric acid dissolves it. 100 parts of cadmium unite with 28,172 of sulphur, to form a sulphuret of a yellow colour, with a shade of orange. It melts at a white-red heat, and on cooling crystallizes in micaceous plates of the finest lemon-yellow colour, which may prove useful in painting. This metal is obtained in abundance from some of the zinc-works.

XIV. NICKEL.

Nickel is found *native*, alloyed by *arsenic* and *silica*; forming *copper-nickel*, *arseniate of nickel*, and *pimelite*.

1.—*Native nickel* resembles in some degree the ore of copper. Specimens of a yellowish colour inclining to grey, have been found in Pengelly Mine, St. Ewe: the solution in nitric acid is of a fine grass-green colour.

2.—*Copper-nickel*, from Pengelly Mine;—copper red; massive; not crystallized, according to Mr. Michell's analysis, contains

Nickel............50.0
Cobalt......... 0.5
Arsenic........ 47.0
Sulphur....... 2.0

A second variety from the same mine, lead-grey, foliated, resembling compact galena, produced

Nickel.........38
Arsenic.........41
Sulphur.........9
Iron 12

Copper nickel, which is uncommonly heavy, is not of very frequent occurrence in the Cornish mines.

3.—*Arseniate of nickel, nickel-ochre, or oxide of nickel*, is an alloy of nickel and arsenic. Its colour is green; white. It has occurred in the above mine, as a thin coating, or efflorescence. It is very soft. Fusible *per se ;* and exhales an arsenical smoke before the blow-pipe.

4.—*Pimelite*—consists of oxide of nickel 15 —silica 35—alumina 5—water 37—with a trace of lime and magnesia. It is yellowish-green; massive; infusible; feels unctuous; occurs in serpentine. Oxide of nickel gives to fluxes a yellow colour. Copper and nickel are both ductile ; they combine readily ; and the alloy is brittle.

XV. COBALT.

Cobalt is found combined with *oxygen*, and with the *sulphuric*, and *arsenic*, acids; and alloyed with *sulphur* and *arsenic*, forming

Oxide
Sulphate
Arseniate } of Cobalt.
Sulphuret
Arseniuret

1.—*Oxide of cobalt :*—It is brown; bluish-black ; grey; when newly broken, steel-grey,

F 3

with a metallic lustre; but it soon becomes tarnished. Its primary form is a cube, the angles and edges of which are frequently truncated; and gradually pass into the octahedron. Cobalt-ore has been found in the copper-lodes of Dolcoath; and accompanying silver in the cross courses of Herland Mine. The cobalt-ore of Huel Sparnon, Redruth, consists of *iron, arsenic, cobalt*, and *copper.* A solid mass of ore of cobalt was brought to the surface at this mine weighing 1333 pounds,

2.—*Sulphate of cobalt*—consists of cobalt 38, sulphuric acid 19, water 14; its colour pale rose-red: it is called *red vitriol.* The regular figure of its crystal is an elongated octahedron exhibiting a prism.

3.—*Arseniate of cobalt*—consists of cobalt 39, arsenic acid 38, water 23. Its colour is red—similar to the peach-blossom, occurring in a fine efflorescence and crystallized. It has been found in Huel Unity, Dolcoath, Polgooth, Huel Sparnon, Huel Trugo; and of an earthy red, occasionally of a bright red, in Botallack. It occurs also with axinite in the slate-rocks of Roscommon cliff, St. Just.

4.—*Sulphuret of cobalt*—consists of cobalt 48, sulphur 38, copper 14, and a trace of iron. This contains no arsenic. It is generally white, or tarnished; and occurs in cubical crystals.

Arseniuret of cobalt.—There are two varieties: *white* arseniuret, composed of cobalt 44, arsenic 55, sulphur 0.50, generally crystallized in a cube, which passes into the octahedron; the faces sometimes convex; striated; and the edges and angles truncated: it occurs also amorphous. *Grey* arseniuret never occurs crystallized:—constituents, cobalt 33.10, ar-

senic 43.47, sulphur 20.08, iron 8.02; before
the blow-pipe these give out arsenical vapour;
tinge the borax a smalt-blue, and melt into a
metallic globule.

Oxide of cobalt before the blow-pipe tinges
borax a deep blue. It is soluble in nitric
acid with effervescence; gives a rose-colour,
crystallizes in needle-shaped crystals, which
deliquesce in the atmosphere.

Cobalt is extensively useful in the arts.
When freed by ustulation from its mineralizer,
(for it is reduced to the simple oxide by roasting,) of which arsenic generally forms the
principal part, it is called *zaffre*. This is of
a sooty, or violet hue, and still retains arsenic, which becomes by torrefaction, an acid
strongly combined with the oxide of cobalt;
and it is this which gives the blue or deep
violet colour to glass. The zaffre of commerce contains about one-fifth of the oxide,
the rest is powdered flint, that is, flint ignited
and quenched in water, and thereby rendered
friable.

Zaffre dissolved in muriatic acid is *sympathetic ink*. Writings, with the solution, when
held before the fire acquire a beautiful leek-
green colour. Zaffre, being the only blue that
will stand vitrifaction, mixed with flint or
glass, and melted, forms a purple glass, which,
when ground, is the *smalt*, used by sign-pain-
ters. When fused with one part of silicious
sand and 2½ of potash, it makes a blue glass,
which is reduced by mills to a subtle powder,
and is then the " blue" used by laundresses.
The pure oxide of cobalt when mixed
with fusible matter is used in painting the
blue on Delft, and other immitations of porcelain.

XVI. ARSENIC.

Arsenic is found *native*; combined with *oxygen*; and mineralized by *sulphur*, forming

Oxide
Sulphuret } of arsenic.

1.—*Native arsenic.*—When pure it is bluish white, not unlike polished steel; but, by exposure, it becomes black. It is the softest and among the most combustible of the metals. It fuses readily before the blow-pipe, emitting a garlick smell, and burns with a bluish flame, with a dense white vapour. When sublimed slowly it crystallizes in tetrahedrons. When completely fused and cooled gradually it forms octahedrons.

2.—The pyrites of arsenic is very common in the Cornish mines;—and the oxide is obtained in great abundance from the desiccation of the ores of tin; and which is collected and operated on for white arsenic in the Parish of Perranarworthall. The *white oxide of arsenic*, which is the arsenic of commerce, is often obtained from it. This mineral is sometimes of a yellow colour, which is owing to the ores from which it is obtained containing sulphur. *Pharmacolite*, (see *lime*,) is often confounded with arsenic; they are thus distinguished:—the oxide of arsenic is soluble in water; pharmacolite is not.

When arsenic is heated in any inflammable mixtures, some of them flies off with it; hence, it is a purifier of glass, and a scorifier of metals, but it carries off the metal with it, if not prevented. Arsenic communicates to fluxes a yellow colour.

3.—*Sulphuret of arsenic;—orpiment—*is red, or yellow. *Red orpiment, or realgar*, consists of arsenic 69, sulphur 31. It melts

immediately before the blow-pipe, giving a pale-yellow flame, and arsenical and sulphurous vapours. It occurs massive; or crystallized in octahedrons with scalene triangles.

Yellow-orpiment is composed of arsenic 62, sulphur 38. It is translucent; burns with a blue-white flame. Before the blow-pipe it smokes, melts, and evaporates. This generally contains more sulphur than realgar.

The dangerous powers of arsenic are considerably abated in these compounds of realgar and yellow orpiment. The Chinese form realgar into medical cups, and employ as a purgative, vinegar, or lemon juice, which has stood some time in them. They also make it into vases, &c.

Arsenic, from its disposition to mix with vitrified earthy bodies, enters into combinations where a white colour is required; hence, it is used in the manufacture of glass, to give it more transparency; and in a larger quantity, a milky opacity, as in enamel for glazing delft-ware, and watch dial-plates.

The beautiful twisted scrolls in the stalks of old wine glasses are arsenic.

When heated with water it communicates a poisonous quality sufficient to kill flies.

Tin, which of itself is easily fused, is, by arsenic, rendered more refractory.

The oxide of arsenic combines with the oxide of copper, and forms a fine colour called *vegitable green*. Realgar is used as a pigment.

The white oxide of arsenic and copperas dissolved in water with vegitable alkali and filtered, &c. form a green pigment which is very permanent.

Arsenic is an ingredient in several processes of dyeing. Orpiment—(that sold in the shops is composed artificially of arsenic and sulphur,) when boiled in water with double its weight of quick-lime, forms a liquor which discovers any quantity of lead dissolved in wine. A few drops mixed with pure wine produces a yellow precipitate; but, if adulterated with lead, the precipitate will be dark, brown or black.

Arsenic is the most violent of all the mineral poisons. When taken into the stomach, it is only when it can be procured in substance, that tests can be applied with certainty; for when it has become dissolved in the gastric-fluid their operation is ambiguous. Of several tests we give one. " A little of the " substance obtained, supposing it to be ar- " senic, may be mixed with about an equal " weight of black flux, or half its weight of " charcoal powder, and exposed to a low red- " heat in a glass tube, coated with clay and " sand, and stopped with a plug of clay. The " oxide will be reduced, and the metal being " volatilized, will form a brilliant crust on " the internal surface of the tube. This test " is the most decisive of any; it is indeed per- " fectly so:—but it can only be properly " employed when, at least, a grain of oxide of " arsenic can be operated on." (Murray's Chemistry.)

Though arsenic does not form the basis of any native salts, it combines with the following as an acid,

The Arseniate of Lime, or pharmacolite;
The Arseniate of Lead;
The Arseniate of Copper;
The Arseniate of Iron;
The Arseniate of Cobalt.

XVII. IRON.

Iron, besides being found *native*, is combined with *oxygen*, the *sulphuric, muriatic, phosphoric, carbonic, chromic, arsenic,* and *tungstic,* acids; and is alloyed by *sulphur, arsenic,* and *silica,* forming

Oxide
Sulphate
Muriate
Phosphate
Carbonate
Chromate } *of Iron.*
Arseniate
Tungstate
Sulphuret
Arseniuret
Silicate

1.—*Native iron.*—A mass weighing 1600 lbs. was found in Siberia. Its interstices were filled with a beautiful green glass, which, from its friability, must have been quenched in water while red hot. It appears to have suffered the most violent ebullition; it is all blistered; and many of the bladders are larger than an egg. It is coated with a crust like iron-stone; internally it is malleable. The Siberian Tartars worship the lump as a deity come down from heaven.

Another mass 15 tons weight has been discovered in Paraguay, of similar structure, but not so solid. In these instances, the fusion has been more complete than what can be produced by the best furnaces. All the glassy matter is transparent;—far different from the slag formed in artificial operations. There is no appearance of sulphur. Both were found remote from all traces of habitation.

2.—*Oxide of iron.—Magnetic iron-stone.*

It consists of protoxide of iron 28.4, peroxide of iron 71.86. The primary form is said to be the octahedron. Colour, grey, black. The massive is the native load-stone.

Magnetic oxide of iron occurs in St. Just, and Gluvias, mixed with green chlorite, slate and tin-stone; and mixed with iron-pyrites in Lanlivery, Roach, and St. Stephens. (See *serpentine.*)

Iron Sand.—*Arenaceous magnetic iron-stone.* It consists of oxide of iron 85, oxide of titanium 9, with small proportions of arsenic, silica, and alumina. Colour, black; and strongly attracted by the magnet. It occurs in angular and roundish grains, and in small octahedral crystals. It is found in a diallage rock near Gwinter, south coast of Cornwall.

Specular iron-ore.—It is tarnished like tempered steel; or is pavonine, or columbine; colour, steel grey. It consists of iron 69, oxygen 31. It occurs massive, or crystallized in brilliant rhomboids, differing little from a cube. From its degree of oxidation it is only attracted by the magnet when finely pulverized. It is insoluble in nitric acid. When heated it dissolves in muriatic acid. It has been found in Carnyorth Moor, St. Just, beautifully crystallized in hexahedral plates, octahedrons, and various modifications of the rhomboid. Similar crystals have been found in Parknoweth and Huel Owls; also in rhomboids in Huel Billon; in hexahedral prisms in Huel Owls; in needle crystals stellated in Boscagel Downs; and in mass, called iron-glance, in Botallack, and in Tincroft. It abounds in the island of Elba.

Iron mica.—It occurs in minute shining scales, and consists of peroxide of iron. It is

black. The iron which it affords is sometimes
called *cold shot*; and it is well fitted for cast
ware. It affords about 55 per cent. of iron. It
is crystallized in six-sided tables. The thin
plates appear blood red, when held up to the
light.

Red Iron-stone. It is one of the most common ores. Its varieties are *red-ochre*, which
melts more easily than any other iron-ore;
red hæmatite, and *jaspery iron-ore*. It is
found in all the forms of stalactites, kidney-
form, balls, &c. The fracture fibrous. It consists of peroxide of iron. Jaspery iron-stone
occurs in Botallack, St. Just; and in Maudlin
Mine, Lanlivery.

Reddle, or *red-chalk*:—Brick, or brownish-
red; stains the fingers, and writes easily;
used principally for drawing. It is never
smelted as an ore. It occurs in St. Just.

Hydrate of iron. Brown hæmatite. It consists of peroxide of iron 80, water 15, with
small proportions of oxide of manganese and
silica. It occurs massive, or in pseudo-crys-
tals, with six sided acute-angled pyramids.
This ore contains from 40 to 60 per cent. of
metal. It effervesces before the blow-pipe,
and tinges borax olive-green. The iron is generally in a state of hydrated oxide. Colour
blackish-brown; reddish and ochre-yellow.
Brittle;—found in Botallack and Tincroft
Mines; it is in great abundance at Huel Rowe
Lead Mine, near Helston.

Umber. It is brown; soft; adheres strongly
to the tongue. Falls to pieces in water. It
seems to be a mechanical mixture of oxide of
iron 48, oxide of manganese 20, silica 13,
alumina 5, water 14. It is found in the parish
of Carhayes.

Black iron-ore. Black hæmatite. It is
bluish-black, and grey. It consists of magnesia, iron-stone, alumina, and lime. It occurs
compact, fibrous, and *ochry.* The fibrous is
fusible *per se.* The ochry occurs in St. Just.
It is not found in great abundance in compa-
rison of the red and brown ores of iron.
Red oxide contains nearly twice as much
oxygen as black, in a given portion.

Bog iron-ore. Yellowish-brown with a resinous lustre. It is said to be caused by the
decomposition of rocks, over which water
passes, and which are deposited in marshy
places. It consists of oxide of iron 66, a small
proportion of oxide of manganese, phosphoric
acid 8, and water 28. Its iron cannot be used
for iron-plate, or wire.

Clay iron-stone. It consists of oxide of iron
and silica; and alumina in some varieties. It
becomes black before the blow-pipe. It is found
in small granular concretions, or lenticular,
aggregated into masses in the coal-deposites
of Great Britain. Its colour is grey, or brown.

Argillaceous iron-ore is that which is worked
in South Wales, Shropshire, and at Carron, in
Scotland.

Cronstedite—composed of oxide of iron about
59, oxide of manganese about 3, magnesia 5,
water about 10, silica 22, accompanied by
sparry iron and hexahedral pyrites, it has been
found at Huel Maudlin. The laminæ are thin
and elastic; the powder, leek-green.

Peroxide of iron nearly pure is of a dull,
deep red, which is the natural colour:—if it
be but little oxidated or in the state of a protoxide, the colour is grey, or black. United
with some fixed air it is yellowish, as in carbonate of iron.

3.—*Sulphate of iron.*—*Iron vitriol.* It has an emerald-green colour. It consists of the oxide of iron 25, sulphuric acid 28, and water 45. It is found in lumps, crystallized, and stalactitical. When exposed to the air it loses its transparency, becomes yellow, ochry, and falls into white powder. It originates from the decomposition of iron-pyrites, when the sulphur absorbs oxygen and forms the acid.

Pitchy iron-ore. Greyish-black. Becomes red in water. Oxide of iron 67, sulphuric acid 8, water 25. Lustre resinous. Translucent on the edges.

4.—*Muriate of Iron.*—*Pyrosmalite.* It consists of protoxide of iron 21, protoxide of manganese 21, submuriate of iron 14, silica 35, with a small proportion of lime and water. It is green. Brown. Lamellar. Translucent on the edges: and crystallized in six-sided columns.

5.—*Phosphate of iron.*—Colour, indigo-blue. It consists of oxide of iron 47, phosphoric acid 32, and water. It dissolves readily in acids. It has been found in fine transparent eight sided bottle-green prisms, and embedded in iron-pyrites, in Huel Kind Mine, St. Agnes. It gives a dark-blue streak on paper.

6.—*Carbonate of iron.*—Spathose iron. Its colour is brown, yellowish-brown. It affects the needle. It consists of oxide of iron 66, carbonic acid 34. It is often confounded with *pearl-spar;* because the crystalline form of spathose iron is exactly similar to that of carbonate of lime; it is only when the metallic matter predominates, that it is called spathose iron.

This mineral is abundant in Cornwall. A variety occurs both in the tin and copper-mines, one of the constituent parts of which is magnesia. It consists of groups of rhomboidal crystals. The general colour is yellow, brown, and white, which distinguishes spathose iron. These crystals are transparent. It has been found in the lodes of Botallack, crystallized in circular tables; hexahedral plates and rhomboids. The colour of these varies from greyish-white to deep brown. It has also been found in Huel Owls, and Huel Boulton in six-sided prisms with acute angled triangular terminations. Spathose iron has occured in Huel Towan, St. Agnes, in flat obtuse rhomboids and in the Maudlin Mine, near Lostwithiel, in large six-sided prisms; in lenticular crystals, grouped in nodules; flattened rhomboids, of a light brown with an external darker mammillated appearance:—fibrous specimens were found in Tincroft Mine, of which the mass was striated perpendicularly to the surface. It effervesces in muriatic acid:—before the blow-pipe it gives protoxide of iron which is very attractable by the magnet.

7.—*Chromate of iron.*—It consists of oxide of iron 34, oxide of chrome 43, alumina 20, with a trace of silica. It is black. Infusible per se. (See *Chrome* and *Chromate of Lead.*)

Chrome has been so called in consequence of the colour which it communicates. This mineral owes its peculiar colour to the presence of chrome in the state of an oxide. The spinelle ruby derives its colour from the same in the state of an acid. It is combined with oxide of lead in the red lead-ore of Siberia. Cromate of iron occurs occasionally in the Lizard Serpentine; hence, the magnetic power of some of the Serpentine.

8.—*Arseniate of Iron.—Cube-ore.* It con-

sists of arsenic acid 31, oxide of iron 45, oxide
of copper 9, with small proportions of silica
and water. Fusible before the blow-pipe. It
gives out arsenical vapour. It is translucent.
Its colour is emerald or bottle-green; sometimes brownish-red; or yellowish-red. it is
crystallized in cubes. It occurs in Carharrack
Mine; Huel Gorland; Huel Unity, in Gwennap; and in Botallack, brown and crystallized
in cubes. The cubes lying on one another,
though easily distinguished by an experienced
eye from the light reflected, frequently cannot
be distinguished without a glass.

In 1823, Mr. Michell discovered in Huel
Beam Tin-Mine, near St. Austle, arseniate of
iron of a new crystallization. The crystals
are grass-green, bottle-green, and pale blue.
Their form is a rhomboidal dodecahedron with
brilliant surfaces. The largest of these crystals seldom exceeds the size of the head of an
ordinary pin. Before the flame of the blow-
pipe arsenical vapours are given off, without
affecting the exterior form of the crystal, and
which is rendered of an ocherous brown colour.

This mineral appears to resemble very
closely that of skorodite, both in its elements of composition and structure. It differs
from the cube-ore, just described, as being a
combination only of arsenic acid, with the
oxide of iron.

Skorodite—occurs massive; and some specimens are crystallized in short rectangular
four-sided prisms; while others occur, perfectly
resembling the martial arseniate of copper in
their external character; it is an arseniate of
iron without copper. Its colour is leek-green;
translucent; melts before the blow-pipe with
emission of arsenical vapour into a reddish-

G

brown mass, which, when all the arsenic is driven off, is attractable by the magnet.

9.—*Tungstate of iron;—Wolfram :*—constituent parts, tungstic acid 64, oxide of manganese 22, oxide of iron 13; colour black; deep brown; yields to the knife. Its oxide is yellow; it is the common concomitant of tin in the veins of Cornwall. It occurs massive, opaque, and brittle; and crystallized in rectangular parallelopipids; and in oblique angled prisms in Stenna Gwyn, and in Huel Fanny, near Redruth.

10.—*Sulphuret of iron.—Iron-pyrites.*— This is one of the most abundant minerals. The primitive form is a cube. Sometimes an octahedron. The colour is yellow. It consists of sulphur 53, iron 47. The cubical yellow crystals in slate are pure specimens of iron pyrites. It is the *mundic* of Cornwall. It often strikes fire with steel, with amazing facility. The cubic pyrites contains a greater quantity of sulphur than the magnetical ore. In the Cornish mines iron-pyrites have been found,—a perfect cube,—in two cubes,—in pentagonal dodecahedrons; in cubes with the solid angles deeply truncated;—in dodecahedrons, the solid angles acuminated by three triangular faces and truncated. There is no depth to which mining has been carried where iron pyrites is not found. The substance of fossil shells, especially the "Cornu-ammonis" is frequently pyritical.

Magnetic pyrites. It consists of sulphur 36, iron 64; fusible *per se.* It is yellow; brown. It contains less sulphur and more iron than common pyrites. It affects the magnetic needle. It has been found in the parish of Lanlivery, and Huel Maudlin, near Lostwithiel.

Hepatic pyrites—liver-brown—is a species of magnetic pyrites; very subject to decomposition; crystallized in tetrahedrons and six-stded prisms.

11.—*Arseniuret of iron; mispickel;*—it consists of iron 58.9, arsenic 42.1. Sometimes there is more arsenic than iron. Colour, tin-white; sometimes, yellowish-white; occurs massive, acicular, and crystallized in a right rhombic prism; gives fire with steel, the sparks accompanied with a white smoke.

12.—*Silicate of iron.*—It consists of silica 30, lime 14, oxide of iron 49, with a trace of alumina and oxide of manganese. In appearance it resembles hornblende. Fusible *per se*, and is then attracted by the magnet. It is soluble in muriatic acid. It is amorphous, or crystallized in rectangular four-sided prisms.

Pyrodmalite. It is liver-brown. Crystallized in six-sided prisms. The powder is a light brown. Before the blow-pipe it gives vapours of muriatic acid, and melts into a bead which is attracted by the magnet. It consists of silica 35, oxide of iron 35, oxide of manganese 23, muriatic acid 2, with a trace of lime.

Hedenbergite, so called from Hedenberg who first described it. It occurs in thin layers with calcareous spar. Its surface is often sprinkled with cubic pyrites, and it is intersected by quartz and mica. Silica 40, oxide of iron 35, water 16, lime 3, with small proportions of alumina, oxide of manganese and carbonic acid.

Meteoric iron. It consists of iron 96, nickel 3. It is formed in the atmosphere, and precipitated to the earth in masses. It is generally of a pale steel-grey colour, and covered with a thin brownish crust of oxide of iron.

Uses of iron.—This metal is so abundant, that while others usually run in veins, whole mountains are composed of iron-stone. It is so universally diffused, that the flesh, hair, milk, and blood of animals contain it. Seeds in distilled water have grown to plants containing iron; and it is found in the ashes of vegetables. Sands, clays, waters of rivers, springs, rain and snow, are scarcely ever free from it. Wherever men are associated, the innumerable effects of industry shew the importance of this copious product of nature.

Iron is soluble in all the acids. The sulphuric acid dissolves it most completely, but water must be added. Sulphuric acid alone on it produces sulphureous acid, not inflammable air. The solution of the iron therefore, requires more oxygen than the acid supplies. Water consists of oxygen and hydrogen which is the base of inflammable air; therefore, when water is added to the acid, the air is oxydated and hydrogen gas is produced.

The attractive power of the magnet has always been known. Its *directive* was discovered about the year 1200, when Guyolas, a native of Provence, wrote a poem "Marineta" in praise of the invention; hence, the Fleur-de-lis is always represented on one of the ends of the needle of the compass.

Iron in its oxydated state is mixed in fusion with vitrified earths; the silicious most easily unites with it. The colour which it most readily communicates is green, as that in common bottles. A minute portion of this oxide gives an incipient vitrification to clays in general, which is seen in bricks and tile.

Such bricks are unfit for fire-places, because
an increased heat makes them run into slag.
Few earths are free from iron. No less than
seven distinct colours, besides a great variety
of shades, are observed in substances containing iron, and to the iron in most cases is the
colour to be attributed;—white in the somnite; black in the obsidian; green in the
euclase: blue in the lazulite: red in the garnet
and ruby; yellow in the topaz; brown in the
tourmaline. To it the emerald, the sapphire,
the amethyst, and the beryl, owe their colours.

Carbonate of iron is found in solution in
chalybeate waters. The oxide of iron is rendered soluble by an excess of carbonic acid.
By adding a few grains of quicklime to a
small quantity of such water, the lime will
combine with the acid, and the oxide of iron
will be precipitated. Iron in mineral waters
is instantly discovered by a tincture of any
vegetable astringent, which strikes a purple
or black colour, according to the quantity of
iron. The tincture of galls either in spirit of
wine or water is generally used.

The infusion of any vegetable containing
tannin, such as sloes, the leaves and bark of the
oak, but especially nut-galls, thrown into a
solution of iron, in any acid, becomes dark
blue or black. Astringents even unite with
iron themselves. If a little infusion of green
tea be spilled on a knife, the astringent principle acts on the iron, and dissolves a minute
portion of it, which becomes of an inky black-
ness. If a knife be laid on a wet oaken table,
it is stained black.

The black colour given to silk, wool, &c.
is occasioned by the combination of the astringent matter with the sulphate of iron.

No other solution of iron, but the sulphate, forms with nut-galls so intense a colour, to render ink permanently black.

A superabundance of astringent matter in the fluid should be present in order to counteract the disposition of the iron to a further oxidation, and prevent the ink from becoming brown. Gum-arabic serves to keep the tannet of iron in suspension, and acts also as a kind of varnish to defend the composition from the action of the air.

The corruption of the vegetable astringent, and the formation of mould on the surface, are retarded by a small quantity of cloves.

The beautiful pigment, called Prussian blue, is a combination of the prussiate of potash, with oxide of iron.

Phosphate of iron is used as a pigment, principally in water-colours : mixed with oil, the colour is a blue, or black : beautiful green and olive colours have been formed by mixing it with other colours.

The combination of iron with carbon exists in nature under the name of plumbago, or black lead. Steel is refined iron combined artificially with carbon. A bar of iron covered with charcoal, exposed to a strong heat increases in weight, and comes out steel. Steel, made red hot and suddenly cooled, acquires such extraordinary hardness as to cut iron, and even softer steel itself. Files sometimes are hardened to such a degree as to break by a fall. Steel, in this brittle state, is fitted for different purposes, by heating it again. When dipped in water it acquires a straw-colour, it is fit for the edges of chisels and punches to be employed on iron; when it acquires incipient purple streaks, it is fit for chisels for the softer metals; a fuller purple prepares it for common edge tools; and the deep-blue or violet, for watch-springs. There is an easier method, by covering pieces of steel with oil or tallow; the different shade of smoke indicates the degree of heat; by this a number of pieces may be done at once.

The surface of a piece of iron can be made steel, and stopped before penetrating through the whole; a paste of horn—or the charcoal of animal substances—covers the iron and is wrapped in clay; in less than two hours, the iron comes out superficially steeled. The steel of gun-locks is thus made.

The fiery sparks produced by the collision of flint and steel are fragments torn off by the flint. By the violence of the stroke, they are heated red hot; they brighten as they recede, and are brightest when at some distance. They are blown up into inflammation when passing through the air. Sometimes a spark is not seen until at a distance. It is owing to this inflammation that sparks kindle gun-powder. Were they nothing more than red hot, they would cool in their passage and fail in setting it on fire.

All iron contains charcoal, and a certain portion of oxygen, which gives it hardness, and without which, iron would be a soft metal. To the different proportions of these two substances are owing the different qualities of iron.

Iron, at a high temperature, readily imbibes charcoal. The compound of charcoal and iron is the substance which flies off in brilliant sparks from iron of a white or high red heat, when struck by the hammer on the anvil; or from those masses which have undergone reduction at the Foundry.

Red hæmatite, when ground, is used for polishing tin, silver, and gold vessels; and for colouring iron brown. Umber is used as a pigment. Reddle is used for drawing: the finer varieties by the painter; the coarser by the carpenter. It is used either in its natural state, or pounded, mixed with gum, and cast into moulds. The crayons for delicate drawing, are mixed with a good proportion of gum, to give them hardness; those for coarser lines, with a smaller quantity.

Different pieces of iron, heated to a red heat, unite perfectly by hammering, or are *welded*. Some silicious sand is thrown into the fire; the sand melts, by uniting with the oxidated metal, and forms a liquid glazing, which prevents farther oxidation. It flies from between the pieces when hammered.

Gun-barrels are rubbed over, when finished, with aquafortis, or muriatic acid, diluted with water, and laid by for a fortnight, till a complete coat of rust is formed. A little oil is then applied, and the surface polished by a little bees' wax. They are then *browned*.

Iron-moulds, occasioned by washing ink-spots with soap, are generally removed by lemon-juice, or oxalic-acid.

Platinum will fuse in contact with steel, at a heat, at which the steel itself is not affected.

Equal parts of platinum and steel form a beautiful alloy, which takes a fine polish, and does not tarnish; the colour is excellent for mirrors.

The medicinal preparations of iron and chalybeate waters, when properly administered, prove friendly to life. They excite a brisker circulation; inspire vigour and alacrity; impart a more healthy colour to the wan countenance; diffuse a general warmth

over the whole system; and exercise an astonishing power in recruiting exhausted nature.

XVIII. TIN.

1.—*Tin* is found combined with *oxygen*, and
mineralized by *sulphur* and *silica*, forming

> *Oxide*
> *Sulphuret* } *of tin.*
> *Silicated oxide*

Oxide of Tin, or *Tin-stone*, is found in most
of the mining districts of Cornwall. The
parish of St. Agnes takes precedence; in that
of St. Just it is next most prevalent. It consists of tin 77, oxygen 21, with small proportions of iron and silica. It is blackish-brown;
gives sparks with steel; decrepitates before
the blow-pipe. When crystallized, it is
usually an imperfect or obtuse octahedron.
The crystals generally are very irregular, and
every vein produces different varieties. Haüy
states their primary form to be a cube; and
Romé de Lisle makes it an octahedron. The
octahedron is composed of two four-sided pyramids, applied base to base. This primary
form, however, never occurs. Crystals have
been found in about 130 varieties. Specimens
of the four-sided prism with the pyramid
have been found in Huel Maudlin, near Lostwithiel; Huel Owls; and in the rocks below
that mine, long four-sided pyramids, without
the prism, have occurred. Tin-crystals are
black, splendent, and generally translucent.

Oxide of tin occurs in Huel Vor of a brownish-black, but more frequently of a jet-black
colour; opaque, with some degree of exterior
splendency, found coating cavities in the

vein, and not unusually on, or mixed with, an inside lining of chlorite; crystallized in quadrangular prisms, terminated by four-sided pyramids, varying in size from acicular, to about $\frac{1}{8}$th of an inch in diameter.

In 1824, tin-stone, raised at Huel Wrath, between St. Ives and Penzance, was covered with small black-splendent crystals, lying in all directions; between them and over the matrix were scattered white acicular crystals, not well perceived, except through a glass.

Small tin-crystals are sometimes found sprinkled on quartz-crystals: they seem to have been drifted only in one direction, as on the back of the quartz columns there are none.

Tin-crystals cemented with chlorite in argillaceous slate have been found in St. Agnes.

Tin-ore has often been found in small reniform pieces rounded, resembling the colour and appearance of a piece of wood cut from a knotted tree; hence, it is called *wood-tin.* It is generally hair-brown. It is very scarce. It consists of oxide of tin 91, oxide of iron 9. It is not reducible to the metallic state before the blow-pipe. It affords 73 per cent. of tin. It has been found in many of the stream-works of the County. It consists of three varieties, viz. *fibrous, compact,* and *dog-tooth.* A variety has lately been found in Tregurthy Moor, consisting of round pebbles of fibrous oxide, the fibres radiating from a centre. These spherical masses are in a rock of schorl and quartz, and their veins pass through decomposed granite. It is called *toad's-eye tin*

Stream-tin has been found in transluscent grains, rolled in garnet, and mixed with tourmaline, at Dartmoor. Garnet coloured tin-stone, and tin-pebbles intermixed with schorl, occur at Luxilian.—Tin, in compact schorl, occurs in Huel Vor. Auriferous tin-stone, composed ol tin, particles of gold, and magnetic iron-stone, has been found in Lanlivery, and in the parish of Kenwyn.

2.—*Sulphuret of tin.*—*Tin-pyrites.*—Its colour approaches that of grey copper-ore, or it is between steel-grey and brass-yellow. It yields easily to the knife. It has been found in Cornwall in Huel Rock, St. Agnes; Stenna Gwyn, St. Stephens; Huel Scorrier, Gwennap; in Botallack, St. Just; and also in the Cronebane mines, Ireland. It has been called *bell-metal ore.* About 40 years ago, in Huel Rock, there was a vein of this ore from 3 to 5 inches wide, and 20 yards beneath the surface. Mr. Raspe, at that time residing in the county, first discovered its composition. Klaproth analyzed it, and found it to contain

Tin........26
Copper.....30
Sulphur....30
Iron........12
Loss........ 1

3.—*Silicated Tin*—is frequently found. Silicated oxide of tin from Huel Primrose, St. Agnes. Found in the state of an impalpable powder, without lustre or cohesion, feels fine, but meagre, and also in a very compact form, and of considerable hardness; colour, yellowish-white and cream-yellow; before the blowpipe on charcoal, becomes yellowish-brown, and is not reduced. According to Mr. Michell's analysis, it consists of

Peroxide of tin.....53.0
Silica 46.0

Muriate of tin.—Muriate of tin was first discovered in a specimen of Jews'-House tin,—which is the antient remains of decomposed tin, smelted by the Jews.—It was found in a low boggy ground, in the Parish of Kea, accompanied with a stratum of charcoal. It was presented to Mr. Gregor by Mr. J. Michell. A vein of saline matter pervaded the mass, which Mr. Gregor found to be muriate of tin. The mass was in a state of decomposition. Pieces of this description have all been found in swampy ground, where sulphuretted hydrogen gas is supposed to be generated. The muriate of tin is almost totally soluble in distilled water.

Jews'-House Tin is the metal of Tin in a state of decomposition, occasioned by its having been long buried under the surface of the earth, and subsequent exposure to the action of air. This very curious production frequently exhibits, in the same piece, three distinct stages of decomposition; the nucleus is of a light steel-grey, with a metallic fracture, easily reduced to powder under the hammer: before the blow-pipe, on charcoal, it is reducible to the metallic state. Contiguous to the latter, is the crystalline substance, in thin tabular crystals, of a yellowish-white colour. This substance is a combination of tin with the muriatic acid: there is also a small portion of sulphuric acid present, and most probably sulphuretted hydrogen.

———

Though tin was the only metallic production of Cornwall during the early ages, it is no where recorded that the ore was ever exported. There is no term for it in the latin language. The woods, with which the county was covered, were employed to reduce the metal. When this practice ceased there is clear evidence. In searching for its origin, we are lost in fabulous history.

From charcoal and scoria having been frequently found mixed, in original masses of reduced metal, the process seems to have been to throw the ore on a charcoal fire. In a mine near St. Austle were found, several years ago, about 80 feet under the ground, two blocks of tin, weighing nearly 26 pounds each; and were supposed to be the manufacture of the Jews who engrossed the whole in the reign of King John. In the Museum of the R. Institution of Cornwall there are two slabs of this description. One of grain-tin was found on the Barton of Carnanton Parish of Mawgan in Pydar; it was discovered two feet and a half under the surface, in swampy ground, and contiguous to what is usually called a Jews' House.

The idea of a reverberatory furnace* was too refined for these simple ages. The great demand for the metal was the cause of the whole mining districts in the four western hundreds being ravaged of their woods; and when the price of tin had become enhanced by the great expence of bringing materials from a distance, and indeed when every coppice had been cut down, except those in the eastern part of the county, a patent was obtained in the second year of Queen Anne, for smelting the ore with Welch-coal.

Stream tin-ore is found only in alluvial soils,

* The first reverberatory furnace for the reduction of tin-ore, was erected on the estate of Newham, near Truro, about the year 1705, by a German Chemist, named Moult. After remaining there a few years, the establishment was transferred to Calenick. There are now about eleven tin smelting houses in the County.

and is disengaged from earthy matter, by the simple application of water. Its reduction is effected in a blast furnace, in conjunction with charcoal. The metal is known in commerce by the name of *grain tin ;* and is, from its superior quality, sold for 10 or 12 shillings per hundred, more than that which is reduced in a reverberatory furnace.

Tin-ore obtained from the mines, is generally found mixed with a variety of extraneous matter, such as wolfram, the arsenical and sulphuretted ores of copper, iron, cobalt, lead, zinc, carbonates of bismuth and iron, together with earthy matter. Previous to its reduction the ore is pulverised in a stamping mill, to various degrees of fineness, depending on the size of its crystallization, and the ingredients with which it is found mixed. If it contains no volatile matter, it is seldom desiccated; on the contrary, this process is never dispensed with. This operation most commonly gives the ore a topaz or garnet coloured appearance. The ore is reduced in a reverberatory furnace, mixed with a portion of culm, and the heat is given by Welch coal. The charge is from 15 to 20 cwt.

At, say, the east end of the furnace is a " ridge" or raised line across the floor ; between that and the eastern wall is the fire : the chimney is at the west end, and its mouth about two feet above the level of the ore, so the heat passes over the whole most intensely : as it melts, the combustible and earthy matter being specifically lighter floats on the surface. By introducing an iron rake, the brilliant metal momentarily meets the eye, below the buoyant covering. In about six hours the metal is let out, and the floor remains covered with scoria. This matter is drawn out at the west end; when cooled it is black from the prevailing oxide of iron. The mode of purifying tin from its alloys differs little from that observed in refining copper.

The tin smelted at the different houses, is cast into moulds, containing about 3 cwt. and while in a fluid state it receives the stamp of the particular house, where it is smelted, thence it is denominated *block-tin*. The blocks are weighed, numbered, and sent to the nearest coinage-town to be *coined*. They are carried into the Coinage-Hall, where a piece of about 3 or 4 ounces is cut off from one of the lower corners, in order to prove the fineness of the metal. The face of the block is then stamped with the Duchy seal, which constitutes the coinage, and is a permit for the owner to sell, and at the same time, the corner being cut off, is an assurance that the tin has been properly examined, is pure, and merchantible. For many years, on an average, the tin has produced to the Duke of Cornwall £10,000 per annum. The value of the whole tin, on an average, amounts to £260,000, of this the proprietors of the soil receive from one-eighth to one-tenth.

The specific gravity of tin, is 7.291, or about 516 pounds to the cubit foot, and although this is less than that of any other malleable metal, and its lightness is a test of its purity, its oxide is the heaviest of all metallic ores; and when mixed in due proportion with all the metals, except antimony, the specific gravity of the mixture is much greater than that of the ingredients. Its component parts are oxide of tin and iron; the latter ingredient generally constitutes the colouring matter, and which almost always accompanies it. Tin is the most fusible of the metals, and when large quantities are melted and allowed to congeal without disturbance its parts concrete into oblong angular prisms.

Uses of Tin.—The metal obtained from stream tin-ore, being the purest, is chiefly used, as moisture has little effect upon it, in coating *sheet-iron.* The plates are cleansed from impurities by steeping in some weak acid, scoured bright, and dipped into melted tin, the surface being covered with suet. The plates are presently covered with the metal. One pound covers 28 square feet. The metal obtained from stream-tin one is also used in the state of chloride as an essential mordant in the *scarlet,* and others of the finest dyes. A tradition prevails, that this was first discovered by webs, or yarn, stained with the ancient purpura, having been boiled in tin cauldrons; and from this circumstance, alone, the dye became fixed.

Tin, in the fluid state, incessantly stirred, until it be congealed, becomes reduced into small grains like sand: this is *powder of tin,* and is used as a remedy to kill worms in the human body.

The surface of copper scraped and washed with a solution of sal ammoniac, and heated, and melted tin flowed over it, becomes tinned. If to blacken the fingers, the tin has been adulterated with lead.

The best sort of *pewter* consists of 100 parts of tin, and all of antimony. For common pewter 5 parts of lead are added. *Putty,* or the oxide of tin elutriated, is used to polish glass and metals, and it solders lead. Tin improves the sonorousness of gold, silver, copper and brass, but it deprives them

of their ductility. Its very vapour renders
gold and silver brittle.

The oxide of tin cannot be vitrified by itself, and with difficulty with vitrifiable bodies;
hence, mixed with the ingredients of glass, and
a little lead, it forms one of the best white
enamels.

Aurum musivum is a combination of tin
and sulphur, and is used for giving a golden
colour to small statue or plaster figures.

Saddlers and harness-makers, for ordinary
uses, cover their wares with tin.

XIX. MOLYBDENUM.

Sulphuret is the only ore of the metal at
present known. It is lead-grey, or like lead
newly cut. Its streak on porcelain is greenish; on paper, bluish-grey. It feels unctuous.
It is nearly malleable. Gives a sulphurous
odour, with a white smoke, before the blow-
pipe. Effervesces in carbonate of soda. It
is massive, and in flat hexahedral tables, and
in six-sided prisms terminated by six-sided
pyramids. It consists of molybdena 60, sulphur 40. It has been found in Drakewalls
mine, near Calstock; Huel Unity and Huel
Gorland, traversing granite. The sulphuret
of molybdena is sometimes incrusted with the
oxide, which is yellow. This *oxide* or *acid* in
a state of saturation, combined with lead, is
molybdate of lead.

The metal molybdenum has only been obtained with great difficulty in small detached
globules; in a blackish-brilliant mass. They
are grey and brittle. Though difficultly fusible, by heat it is easily converted into a white
oxide, rising in brilliant needle-form flowers.

H

Nitric acid readily oxidizes, and ultimately converts it into molybdic acid. This acid, in its action on metals, is decomposed and partly reduced to the state of an oxide. By adding solutions of alkaline molybdates to the solution of different metallic salts, the molybdic acid is precipitated, combined with the metallic oxide, and several rich colours are obtained. That obtained from muriate of tin is a fine blue; and, if fixed in cloth as a dye, may be durable. The molybdates added to vegetable dyes give a permanency to the colours.

XX. ANTIMONY.*

Antimony is found *native*, combined with *oxygen*, and mineralized by *sulphur*, forming

Oxide
Sulphuret } *of Antimony.*

1.—*Native Antimony*—is of a tin-white, and becomes, on exposure to the air, of a yellowish-black colour. It occurs massive, and crystallized in an octahedron: lustre, splendent, and metallic: yields to the knife. Klaproth's analysis is—antimony 98, silver 1, iron 0.25. It melts easily by the blow-pipe; and the reduced bead of metal, on cooling slowly, becomes covered with brilliant acicular crystals.

2.—*Oxide of Antimony;—White ore of antimony;*—found sometimes in quadrangular tables and cubes; sometimes in acicular crystals grouped like zeolite; and in prisms; colour white, and yellowish white. This ore is a pure

* *Antimony*, we are told by authors, received its name from the following circumstance. Basil Valentine, a German monk, having thrown some of it to the pigs, observed, that, after it had purged them violently, they immediately grew fat. This made Basil think, that, by giving a like dose to his fellow monks, it would also fatten them. Worthy Basil's experiment failed; and the whole brotherhood died to a man. Hence, the name *anti-monk.*

oxide of the metal. *Red ore* of antimony—occurs in capillary crystals grouped together; colour, cherry red; contains oxide of antimony 78, sulphur 19.

3.—*Sulphuret of antimony*. The most common state of antimony is a combination of sulphur;—antimony 74, sulphur 26;—but it is often associated with other minerals, such as arsenic, iron, nickel, copper, silver, lead, &c.— The sulphuret has been found in about twenty varieties of form:—its crystallized prism is a rhomboid.

To say, that the specimens are full of long, shining, needle-shaped striæ, or consist of dark bluish filaments parallel to each other, is giving no idea of their exquisite texture. One, of the thousands of specimens to be seen in Cornwall, will give a more clear idea of the crystallization than any abstract description.

Radiated *grey ore* of antimony from Port Isaac; colour, lead-grey; crystallized in four-sided prisms, surface of the crystals longitudinally striated, contains, according to Mr. Michell's analysis,

Antimony.... 68.15
Lead 1.5
Sulphur...... 26.0
Silica........ 3.0
                ———
                98.0

Compact grey ore of antimony from the parish of St. Merrin; colour, dark lead-grey; fracture fine grained, analized by Mr. Michell,

Antimony..... 54.0
Copper 14.0
Iron 3.5
Sulphur...... 27.5

The compact variety has also been found at St.
German's; plumose, at Endellion:—it has also
been found at St. Stephens; Huel Boys mine,
near Padstow, once produced 100 tons a year,
containing 8 parts in 20 of pure antimony.

The metal is brittle; of a scaly texture;
destitute of malleability, and easily beaten
into powder. When fused before the blow-
pipe, its white smoke condenses on any cold
surface. This is partly an oxide formed by
the action of the air. When cooling, the vapour condenses on the metal itself, like a
covering of snow. In sulphuric acid assisted
by heat, it froths and runs over the vessel
amidst fumes of sulphurous acid; and at last,
comes actual sulphur.

Oxide of antimony combines with oxide of
lead, and forms the paint, *Naples-yellow*.

Oxide of antimony promotes the vitrification
of some earths, and gives the glass a hya-
cinthine color.

Antimony is used in refining gold; to
harden tin and lead in the composition of
pewter; in bell-metal to make the sound more
clear; to give a finer texture to the composition of specula, or burning concaves; and in
the casting of cannon balls, by helping the
fusion of the metal.

It is used in the greatest quantity in letter
founding. The latent heat necessary for the
fluidity of this composition is very moderate;
so that persons can work without intermission.
The mould loses so much heat while opening to
shake out the letter, and shutting it again, that
the next letter makes no accumulation of heat.

XXI. TELLURIUM.

It is found only *native*, and combined with
gold, silver, lead, or iron.

Native Tellurium is of a white shining colour. It occurs in minute crystals, or massive. It is volatilized before the blow-pipe,
in a dense white vapour. It consists of tellurium 90, with small proportions of gold and
iron.

Graphic Tellurium consists of tellurium 60,
gold 30, silver 10. It is found aggregated on
quartz, crystallised in minute prisms. Its
colour steel-grey; of a metallic lustre; of an
uneven fracture; and becomes tarnished in the
air.

Yellow, or *white Tellurium.* It is crystallized in minute four-sided prisms, or disseminated. The colour is white, inclining to
yellow. Its fracture is foliated. It consists of
tellurium 44, gold 26, lead 19, silver 8. It is
worked on account of its gold.

Black Tellurium. Fusible *per se.* Occurs
in plates, or in six-sided tables, somewhat
elongated, the leaves slightly flexible. The
principal constituent parts, tellurium 32, lead
54, gold 9, with a small proportion of sulphur,
copper, and silver. It stains slightly. It is
worked both for gold and silver. It melts
before ignition, at a heat a little higher
than what melts lead, and is as volatile as
arsenic. It inflames before the blow-pipe,
with a vivid blue light-green on the edges,
and is dissipated in greyish-white vapours, which condense into a white oxide.
It is easily dissolved by the acids. It is
obtained in small quantities; and its use is
very little.

———

XXII. ZINC.

Zinc—is combined with *oxygen*, the *sul-*

B 3

phuric and *carbonic* acids, and mineralized by *sulphur* and *silica*, forming

$$\left.\begin{array}{l} \textit{Oxide} \\ \textit{Sulphate} \\ \textit{Carbonate} \\ \textit{Sulphuret} \\ \textit{Silicate} \end{array}\right\} \textit{of Zinc.}$$

Zinc is not found native.

1.—Red *oxide* of zinc occurs in various shades, which are supposed to be owing to the presence of oxide of iron. It is massive; opaque; translucent on the edges. It burns dull when exposed to the air. It is infusible *per se.* It consists of zinc 76, oxygen 16, with small proportions of manganese and iron.

2.—*Sulphate of Zinc;—White vitriol;—*It is found in the state of powder, tubular, or crystallized. The crystals are rhomboidal octahedrons. It is greyish, reddish, yellow, or greenish-white. Translucent. It dissolves in boiling water, and intumesces before the blow-pipe. It consists of oxide of zinc 27, a trace of oxide of manganese, sulphuric acid 22, water 50. It is formed by the decomposition of *blende*, which becomes acidified by the absorption of oxygen, and thus forms sulphuric acid, and which, combining with the oxide, forms the sulphate.

3.—*Carbonate of Zinc;—Calamine;—*It consists of oxide of zinc 65, carbonic acid 34. It is hardly distinguishable from limestone, than which it is twice as heavy. It dissolves with effervescence in sulphuric acid. It is infusible *per se.* Its colour is yellowish, white, or brown. It occurs both massive and crystallized, and is generally combined with a large portion of silex.—*Hydrous carbonate*; oxide of zinc 71.4, carbonic acid 13.5, water 15.1.

Colour, white; form, stalactitical. Before the blow-pipe becomes yellow; dissolves with ef-fervescence in sulphuric acid, and when heated loses about ¼ of its weight.

3.—*Sulphuret of zinc;—Blende.* It consists of zinc 64, sulphur 20, with small proportions of iron, fluoric acid, &c. Its varieties are *yellow blende* of an adamantine lustre; massive, and crystallized in four-sided prisms; frequently semi-transparent; found at Trenarron, in St. Austle; and Huel Briggan, Perranzabuloe.— *Brown blende;* the most common occurs translucent in tetrahedrons, octahedrons, rhomboidal dodecahedrons, and octahedrons with an intermediate four-sided prism; it has been found in St. Agnes; Baldhu, parish of Kea; and Huel Fortescue, Gwennap. Sul-phuret of zinc, in stalactitical and mamillated forms,—occurs in Huel Unity, Gwennap; Huel Wentworth, Redruth; and Lanescot Mine, in Tywardreath. Colour varies from ash-grey to dark brown; fracture close grain-red; inclines to resinous. Soluble in nitric acid with effer-vesence; and emitting sulphuretted hydrogen. A mamillated specimen from Huel Unity pro-duced according to Dr. Kidd, oxide of zinc 67, sulphur 33. Proust is of a contrary opinion; and so is Thomson;—from the experiments made by Mr. Michell on this sulphuret, he is of opinion that it is the *metal* of zinc combined with sulphur. Its lustre is splen-dent, inclining to resinous. *Black blende,* consists of zinc 53, iron 12, sulphur 26, &c. It is black; brown; or red with a metallic lustre. Infusible *per se.* Massive, and crys-tallized. Mostly opaque. It occurs frequently in the tin and copper veins of Cornwall; it has been found distinctly crystallized in St. Agnes.

The *yellow* variety is thought to be pure; the *brown* and *black*, to contain more or less oxide of iron. It is called " Black Jack."

5.—*Silicate of zinc ;—Electric calamine ;— Silicious oxide of zinc ;*—It consists of oxide of zinc 75, silica 25, and water. It is soluble without effervescence in muriatic acid. It is grey; blue. The crystals are minute and indistinct. It occurs with blende, galena, and sulphuret of copper. It decrepitates and shines with a green light before the blow-pipe. Cadmium, a new metal, has been lately discovered in some of the silicates and carbonates of zinc.

Uses of zinc. Zinc, of all metallic bodies, except manganese, seems to unite most readily with oxygen, and often causes inflammation at the moment it seizes it,—taking it from almost every other body ;—hence, its importance in chemical operations.

Zinc in fine filings mixed with gunpowder, produces the brilliant stars in fire-works.

Zinc is one of the metals used in galvanism.

Zinc and copper while being acted on by acids become *magnetic*, as is beautifully exemplified by an instrument lately invented, (now standing before the author,) which consists of a small cylindrical galvanic aparatus, balanced on a perpendicular magnet :—the moment the action of the acid on the metals commences, the zinc and copper plates begin to revolve in opposite directions, which motion continues as long as the action of the acid continues.

Four parts of mercury and one of zinc form the most powerful amalgam for the electrical machine,

Zinc affords, with copper, brass of high malleability, of fine colour, which is used in the most delicate workmanship. It melts long before ignition; soon after it becomes red hot, it burns with a dazzling white flame of a bluish or yellowish tinge, and is oxidized with such rapidity, that it flies off in the form of white flowers, called *philosophical wool.*

Calamine and charcoal are put in deep pots; set in a furnace; their mouths are stopped; the metallic vapour issues through iron tubes, which pass through the bottom of the pots, and is condensed in small particles in water; and melted into ingots. Spelter, as sold in London, in a granulated form, is used for soldering by braziers.

Zinc sticks in the files when working, and renders them useless: lead, though a much softer metal, has not this quality. When mixed with copper, which has the same quality, it forms a compound which can be more pleasantly worked than any other metal.

When neutralized by sulphuric acid, it produces *white vitriol*, which is used to remove inflammation of the eyes, &c. A fine colour called *zinc-white*, superior to white lead, is made from it. This colour is prepared by dissolving sulphate of zinc in water; and the zinc-white, or oxide, is precipitated by potash, or chalk.

It is owing to the virtue of zinc as a component of brass, that pins are coated with tin. The method is thus performed; a vessel is filled by layers of brass-pins, and plates of tin, one of which plates being uppermost and another below, the vessel has then a solution of cream of tartar poured in; the acid dissolves the tin, which the zinc of the brass precipitates on them in a metallic state, by which, after a few hours boiling, they are uniformly tinned.

XXIII. MANGANESE.

Manganese is found in the state of an *oxide*, and combined with *carbonic* and *phosphoric* acids, and mineralized by *sulphur* and *silica*, forming

Oxide
Carbonate
Phosphate } of Manganese.
Sulphuret
Silicate

Oxide of Manganese. The *grey oxide* is found in great abundance in Cornwall, viz.—*Radiated*, colour steel grey, crystallized in four-sided prisms, their faces longitudinally striated. *Foliated*, steel-grey; crystallized in rhombs. *Compact*; steel-grey, massive. *Earthy grey-ore*; dark steel-grey.. It consists of oxide of manganese about 90, oxide of iron 10. All the varieties have the same chemical character. They are not melted before the blowpipe; but assume a brown colour. To borax they communicate a violet-blue.

Black oxide;—very rare; found frequently mixed with grey antimonial ore. Colour between brownish and greyish-black; massive, crystallized in octahedrons. It is called "Wad," which becomes red hot when mixed with oil, and exposed to the air;—consists of oxide of manganese 43, oxide of iron 43, with small proportions of silica or lead. It has been found in Pednandrae mine, Redruth.

Red oxide;—massive; pale ruby-red; cherry-red. It has been found in Creva Wood, near Callington; Trebartha; Indian Queens; and Veryan.

2.—*Carbonate of Manganese;*—Rose-red; translucent; composed of small aggregated crystalline masses. It consists of oxide of manganese 48, carbonic acid 40, oxide of iron 2, and a trace of silica.

3.—*Phosphate of manganese.* It is raven-black. It consists of oxide of manganese 42, phosphoric acid 27, oxide of iron 31. It scratches glass; massive; opaque; the thin fragments are translucent; fuses easily and intumesces *per se* before the blow-pipe.

4.—*Sulphuret of manganese.* It is brownish-black. Occurs massive. Consists of oxide of manganese 82, sulphur 11, carbonic acid 5. Found in Cornwall.

5.—*Silicate of manganese ;*—Rose red; massive; opaque; it scratches glass and strikes fire with steel; the thin splinters are translucent. It consists of peroxide of manganese 52, silica 39, oxide of iron 4, with a trace of lime and water. It has been found in the neighbourhood of Callington.

The oxide of manganese occurs in small quantity in a number of other minerals; it exists in the vegetable kingdom, being found generally in the ashes of plants.

It is from the grey oxide, that most of the oxygen-gas used by the chemist is obtained.

Manganese combines, perhaps, with a greater portion of oxygen than any other metal, and parts with most of it again, by the mere application of heat in close vessels. This it communicates to acids, particularly the muriatic acid, when distilled over it, which causes it to escape in oxymuriatic gas, or acid. This deprives most vegetable substances of their colour, both in the state of gas, and also when mixed with water, by which it is absorbed; hence, its use in bleaching linen, and rags for the manufacturing of paper; but it being found that the gas destroyed the stuff, this effect was mitigated by combining it with pure potash dissolved in the same water by which it was absorbed. From *grey ore* of manganese chlorine is now obtained by distillation, with muriatic acid, or with a mixture of sulphuric acid, common salt and water; the latter is generally the method employed for procuring it on a larger scale, for bleaching, and other arts and manufactures.

When fused with certain earthy or metallic substances, it deprives them of their colour; hence, in glass manufactories, it is employed to remove the green colour of common glass; and it gives the black colour to certain black earthenware.

Added in small quantity to glass, it destroys the brown colour caused by intermixed inflamable substances, or, in greater quantity, it gives it a violet colour.

It affords a fine brown-colour, used for painting on porcelain.

It is used at every potter's kiln to give the dark glazing to the coarsest earthenware.

It is used for tinging glass purple, and to compose the enamels used in decorating the glazing of some earthenware, such as the tiles with which fire-places were formerly lined.

The oxides of other metals are always of the deepest colour when the greatest quantity of oxygen has been taken from them, but manganese becomes perfectly white; it recovers its oxygen speedily by being exposed to the air; and it, at the same time, recovers its natural blackish-colour.

The metal is so difficultly fusible that no heat can make it run into a mass of any magnitude. It is applied to no useful purpose. To preserve specimens in a metallic state they

must be varnished, for even the air of a phial
rusts them in a very short time.

XXIV. COLUMBITE.

Columbite, or *tantalite*,—consists of oxide of
tantalum 80, oxide of iron 15, oxide of manganese 5. It is bluish-black; crystallized in
imperfect prisms longitudinally striated; gives
sparks with steel.

Mixed with charcoal, and exposed to a violent heat in a charcoal-crucible the metal columbium is obtained, which is dark grey.
Neither nitric, muriatic, or nitro-muriatic
acid, produces any change on it.

Yttrotantalite;—a variety of the above;
consists of oxide of tantalum 45, oxide of iron
and yttria 55. It is iron-black; grey; brown
and opaque. It is found in small angular
pieces, and crystallized in oblique four and
six-sided prisms.

XXV. CHROME.

The metal *chromium* is extracted from the
native chromate of lead; and from that of iron,
which being most abundant is usually preferred. It is a porous mass of agglutinated
grains; very brittle; and of a colour intermediate between tin and steel.

It is sometimes obtained in acicular crystals,
crossing each other in every direction.

It resists all the acids, except the nitro-muriatic, which at a boiling heat oxidizes it and
forms a dark-green sulphate.

Chromate of mercury is of the colour of
vermilion; chromate of silver, a carmine red;
chromate of zinc and bismuth, a bright
yellow. (See *chromate of iron and lead.*)

Cerium—comprehends
    Cerite, or *silicate of cerium*,
    Allanite,
    Gadolinite,
    Yttrocerite,
    Orthite,
    Fluate of cerium.

1.—*Cerite; silicate, or oxide of cerium*. It is of a rose-red colour, occasionally tinged with clove-brown. It is found massive and disseminated. It is opaque; gives sparks with steel, and gives a greyish-white streak. It consists of oxide of cerium 54, silica 34, with some oxide of iron, lime, water, and carbonic acid. It forms a red glass before the blow-pipe, whose colour fades when cooling.

2.—*Allanite*.—The principal constituent parts are, oxide of cerium 33.9, oxide of iron 25.4, silica 35.4, lime 9.2, alumina 4.1, moisture 4. It is about the hardness of glass, and brittle. Its crystals are four, six, or eight-sided prisms. It is brownish-black; massive; opaque. It froths and melts before the blow-pipe into a black scoria.

3.—*Gadolinite*.—It consists of yttria 16, silica 25, oxide of cerium 17, with some alumina. It intumesces before the blow-pipe, and melts into a magnetical slag. It is velvet black, with a shining lustre.

4.—*Yttrocerite*.—It is greyish-red; greyish-white; violet; amorphous; opaque. Infusible *per se*. With gypsum it is fusible. It consists of oxide of cerium 13, yttria 14, lime 47, fluoric acid 24.

5.—*Orthite*.—It resembles gadolinite. It has been found in granite, and occurs always in straight layers. It consists of protoxide of cerium 19, protoxide of iron 12, protoxide of manganese 8, yttria 3, silica 32, alumina 14, lime 7, water 5. With borax before the blow-pipe it dissolves readily into a red glass, which becomes yellow as it cools.

6.—*Fluate of cerium.*—It is a rare mineral, and so much so, that sufficient specimens have with difficulty been found for a single analysis. It is amorphous; and crystallised in six-sided prisms. Its colour is red. It consists of protoxide of cerium 30, perfluate, or fluate of peroxide of cerium 68, with a trace of yttria.

XXVII. TITANIUM.

This mineral occurs in the following varieties:—

Oxide
{ Menaccanite,
Rutile,
Octahedrite,
Iserane,
Nigrine.
Silicate....Sphene.

1.—Mr. Gregor first discovered titanium. He found it in ferruginous sand in the rivulet flowing through the vale of Menaccan, in Cornwall, which appeared to be the oxide of a new metal, and he called it *menaccanite.* It consists of oxide of iron 51, oxide of titanium 45, with small proportions of manganese and silica. It is iron-black; and in small flattish angular grains, like gunpowder. It is attractable by the magnet, but in a much less degree than iron-sand, or magnetic iron-stone. It is infusible before the blow-pipe, but gives borax a greenish brown.

More lately it has been found in a stream

near Lanarth, in the parish of St. Keverne, adjoining Menaccan. A variety has also been discovered in a diallage rock, near Gwendra, on the south coast of the county. It is infusible *per se*. The acids only extract a little iron from it.

Oxide of titanium was used to give a brown or yellow colour in painting on porcelain, before its nature was known.

2.---*Rutile*.---It is reddish-brown. Blood-red. Slightly translucent. Infusible *per se*. It is a pure oxide of titanium, slightly intermixed with oxide of iron. The crystals six-sided, sometimes four-sided prisms, longitudinally streaked. It is insoluble in acids. It scratches glass. It is found in the slate quarries at Dinyball, in Cornwall, in hair brown-capillary threads perforating quartz crystals in various directions.

3.---*Octahedrite*, or *anastase*. Pyramidal titanium-ore. It is always crystallized. The primary form an elongated octahedron, whose base is a square. Its colour is schorl-blue; indigo-blue; brown. It is strongly transparent. Infusible *per se*. It is an oxide of titanium. It scratches glass. Count Bournon found it crystallized on granite, in Cornwall.

4.---*Iserene*. Found in small angular grains and rolled pices. It consists of oxide of titanium 48, oxide of iron 48, oxide of uranium 4. Its colour is iron-black; opaque. Before the blow-pipe it fuses into a brownish glass which is slightly attracted by the magnet.

5.---*Nigrine*.---It consists of oxide of titanium 84, oxide of iron 14, with a trace of oxide of manganese. It occurs in grains, and is distinguished from manaccanite by its stronger lustre, superior hardness, colour of its streak which is yellowish-grey, or brown, and by its not being magnetic. With borax, without which it is infusible, it melts into a globule of transparent hyacinthine-red.

6.—*Silicate of titanium ;—Sphene ;—Prismatic titanium-ore.*—It consists of oxide of titanium 33, silica 35, lime 33. It is red; yellow; brown; green; lustre, adamantine, resinous or vitrious ; commonly crystallized in four-sided shining prisms a quarter of an inch long. Infusible *per se.* With borax it gives a yellowish-green glass.—Translucent on the edges; scratches glass. Insoluble in acids. It has been found amorphous, and also in rhomboidal octahedrons.

XXVIII, SELENIUM.

Selenium, after fusion, assumes a solid metallic brilliancy, and of the colour of lead. Pulverised, it is a deep red ; when pounded it sticks together, assumes a smooth surface and grey colour like antimony or bismuth. It may be kneaded between the fingers, drawn into long elastic, transparent-threads, which when viewed by transmitted light are red; by reflected light they are grey, and of a metallic lustre.

Sulphur, phosphorus, the earths, and the metals, combine with selenium, forming seleniurets.

It has been obtained in small quantities from large portions of pyrites. (See *seleniuret of silver.*

I

INFLAMMABLE MINERALS.

The class of substances most nearly allied to the metallic are the *Inflammable Minerals,* viz.

1 *Sulphur* is a mineral " sui generis."

2 *Diamond,*
3 *Plumbago,*
4 *Mineral charcoal,*
5 *Anthracolite,*   } composed principally of carbon.
6 *Coal,*
7 *Jet,*
8 *Bituminous wood,*

9 *Naphtha,*
10 *Petroleum,*
11 *Mineral pitch,*
12 *Asphaltum.*
13 *Fossil copal,*   } Liquid Bitumens, composed chiefly of hydrogen and carbon, of which hydrogen predominates.
14 *Retinasphaltum,*
15 *Amber,*
16 *Mellilite,*

I 2

I. SULPHUR.

Sulphur is principally the production of volcanoes. It is characterized by its yellow colour. It is semitransparent; massive; stalactitical; and crystallized in octahedrons and dodecahedrons.

Sulphuric acid, or oil of vitriol, is obtained from this substance by burning it in oxygen-gas in chambers lined with lead, and bringing it to a state of purity by distillation. If heat be applied it decomposes water by uniting with its oxygen; and the hydrogen is let loose in the state of inflammable gas.

Sulphuric and boracic acids are the only two found in a native state.

Sulphur is found in the three kingdoms of nature. The different *pyrites* shew its strong affinity to certain metals. The ores of most contain it. It is generally found in coal.

Relics of animal substances are found completely impregnated with it. The *cornu ammonis* affords striking specimens of this.

Hepatic gas arises from putrid vegetables. The clay of pits where flax has been steeped, for seasons, burns with a blue sulphuric smoke. The juices of several plants, especially that of the dock, contain sulphur.

Sulphur may be separated by any acid from alkaline substances. In the moment of separation a gas is emitted resembling the smell of rotten eggs. The vapour from a boiling egg contains this gas. If an alkaline sulphuret, a boiled egg, or a piece of newly manufactured horn, be shut up in a cupboard, all the plate in it will be tarnished black in a few days.

When melted in a strong heat it becomes thick and viscid; poured into water it is ductile, and is used for taking impressions of medals or seals.

The chief preparation from sulphur is sulphuric acid. But as sulphur burned at a low temperature absorbs less oxygen than when exposed to a greater heat, it is less acidified, and produces *sulphurous* acid. By reducing the temperature of this gas by artificial cold, it becomes liquid; and is absorbed by water.

Mercury, tin, chopped straw, or saw dust, are often employed to abstract part of the oxygen from sulphuric, in order to obtain sulphurous acid. Water saturated with sulphurous acid destroys most vegetable colours. Blues are reddened by it previous to their being discharged. A red rose held over the flame of a match will become variegated, or entirely white, wherever the sulphurous acid comes in contact. The red colour will be recovered gradually by dipping it in water.

Sulphuric acid has a strong attraction for water. It mixes with violence; grows hot; and if not mixed gradually, and by small additions, it will break any glass vessel. When mixing it contracts: 26 measures of water and 4 of acid make only 29 of mixture. It is the great instrument for detecting other acids. It dislodges every one of them. A small quantity diluted, and rubbed on with a rag, will immediately clean tables or desks from ink stains, &c. Its use is extensive in metallurgy, tanning, bleaching, and dyeing. In medicine it is used as a tonic and stimulant; and sometimes externally as a caustic.

With argillaceous earth sulphuric acid forms alum; with calcareous earth, gypsum; with ponderous earth, heavy spar; with magnesia, Epsom salt; with soda, Glauber's salt; with oxide of iron, green vitriol; with oxide of copper, blue vitriol; with oxide of zinc, white vitriol; with oxide of cobalt, red vitriol.

Sulphur is a principal ingredient in gunpowder. (See *Nitre.*)

II. THE DIAMOND.

Charcoal is principally produced from wood in a smothered fire. It is also obtained from other substances containing inflammable matter, as vegetables, animal substances, and bitumens, such as soot, or ivory-black, and lamp-black, &c. which form the basis of black paints, indian ink, and printers' ink. It resists the action of heat, humidity, and the most powerful solvents. The sulphuric, nitric, and phosphoric acids; and the oxides of metals, act upon it when heated in the same way as they affect inflammable bodies. From its powerful affinity for oxygen, it separates it from all other bodies, and reduces the metallic oxides to the metallic state. It decomposes water by attracting its oxygen. It removes the heavy smell of gummed or oiled silks or linen. It instantly removes the dead flavour of spirits distilled from grain. It sweetens putrid water and meat. It is an excellent dentrific : this correction of putrescence is accompanied by a sensible increase of offensive effluvia. It is insoluble in water, hence, the utility of charring the surface of wood exposed to that liquid.

Carbonic acid abounds in nature. It composes 44 parts in 100 of the weight of limestone, marble, and calcareous spar, from which it may be extricated by heat, or by the superior affinity of some acid. Sulphuric acid diluted with 5 or 6 times its weight of water, on chalk, which is a compound of carbonic acid and lime, produces an effervescence, and the carbonic acid is evolved in the state of gas. This acid is nearly twice as heavy as common air, and occupies the lower part of mines or caverns, where decomposing materials produce it.

Carbonic acid is emitted in large quantities during vinous fermentation; and occupies the upper part of the vessels. Lighted paper dipped into it is immediately extinguished; and the smoke remaining on the carbonic acid renders its surface visible, which may be thrown into waves by agitation. A cup of water immersed in this gas, and agitated, becomes impregnated with it, and resembles Pyrmont water. The acid may be lifted out in a pitcher, and bottled. Its peculiar sharp taste is perceptible in sparkling champaign, and brisk cider.

The atmosphere contains a small portion of carbonic acid, as animals and vegetables admit carbon to the number of their constituent parts. As its weight is more considerable than that of common air, it constantly occupies the lowest part of the atmosphere.

Such is the principle existing in charcoal; and which, from its active disposition to combine with almost every substance, is never found pure and unmixed, except the hardest, and most brilliant of all stones,—*The Diamond*, which nature exhibits to a wondering world, in the state of pure native carbon. A diamond, enclosed in iron and exposed to an intense heat, vanishes without any residue, and combining with the metal, converts it into steel.

Charcoal is, then, an oxide of carbon, or the

woody fibre partially oxydized, and consists of diamond 64, oxygen 36. Carbonic acid consists of charcoal 28, oxygen 72, or diamond 18, and oxygen 82, and the diamond is pure carbon, entirely without oxygen. Carbonic acid has been analysed, when its charcoal has been exhibited entire.

The inimitable qualities by which the consent of mankind has fixed an immense value upon this stone, are these. It is the hardest body in nature. It cuts all other substances. It takes an exquisite and lasting polish.* Its refracting power is such as to cause all the light falling on any of its interior surfaces to be reflected at a greater angle of incidence than 24½ degrees. An artificial gem does not reflect the light from its hinder surface, until that surface be inclined in an angle of 41 degrees. The diamond, therefore, not only throws back all the light which an artificial gem can reflect, but one half as much more. This added to its extreme transparency, and the accuracy of its polish when cut into a regular solid, gives it its surprising lustre and beautiful play of colours.

* We read, *Exodus*, ch. 28, that the diamond was one of the gems in Aaron's breast-plate. On this, without venturing on Biblical criticism, it may be observed, that the art of *engraving* diamonds was not known in the times of Moses. In modern times, there is an account of only two " engraves." The one belonged to *Charles* I. and had the arms of Great Britain on it. The other belonged to *Mary* of Austria, Queen of France. Another reason why the diamond may be supposed not to have been in the High Priest's breast-plate is, that the diamond used in a metaphorical sense always means *hostile* or *implacable*; as we read in Æschylus, (*Prometh. vinct. v. 6.*) in Horace, (*Lib. 3. ode 24.*) and in Virgil, (*Æn. Lib.* vi. 552.) But, none of the stones of the *Essen* was intended to suport in the designs of Jehovah, his implacability to the Jews; but all were indicative of the kindness of Providence. Another reason is, there is no mention of the diamond amongst the stones of the New Jerusalem; and that catalogue is evidently taken from the High Priest's breast-plate, for the stones, though with different names, which can be easily reconciled, are the same in both. (See *Doddus* on the Revelation; edition of 1720, p. 996.)

Diamonds, from the east, generally exhibit octahedral crystals, or a double four-sided pyramid. Those from Brazil exhibit dodecahedral crystals, with rhomboidal faces, making a six-sided prism, terminated by two three-sided pyramids. The matrix is generally quartz, white sand, iron-stone, or granite.

The structure of the diamond is lamellar; and can be mechanically divided, according to all the planes of its primary crystal, the regular octahedron.

Being first cleft into lamellæ, it is shaped by being rubbed against other diamonds. It is then polished, by an horizontal steel wheel, dusted with its own powder, mixed with olive oil.

III. PLUMBAGO. BLACK LEAD. GRAPHITE.

Plumbago contains a small quantity of oxygen. It is diamond in its first state of oxidation: charcoal is in the second state of oxidation: carbonic oxide in the third; and carbonic acid, the product of the complete oxidation of carbon.

Plumbago, instead of the earth and salt of common charcoal, has a small quantity of iron for its base. It is a carburet of iron, consisting of carbon 91, iron 9. It is not acted on by acids. When exposed to an open fire, it burns with a reddish flame, and emits beautiful sparks, with a smell of sulphur. During combustion it emits a great deal of carbonic acid, but it burns without flame or smoke, leaving a residuum of red oxide of iron.

The presence of plumbago is exhibited by dissolving steel or crude iron in acids, in which it is insoluble, and therefore remains behind in the form of a powder. Hence, is deduced the cause of the black spot which remains on steel after its surface has been corroded by an acid; for this spot consists of plumbago which continues after the iron has disappeared in solution.

It occurs in lamellar masses and kidney shaped lumps; and sometimes crystallized in six-sided prisms, the summits striated parallel to their edges. The finest kind used for pencils is found at Borrodale in Cumberland. It is boiled in oil; and sawed into slips about 1-10 of an inch thick, which are glued between two slender half-cylinders of cedar. The dust, or refuse of the sawings, is mixed with gum-arabic, or fused with resin, or sulphur, for inferior pencils. The powder of plumbago with thrice its weight of clay and some hair make a coating for retorts. It is also used for preserving grates and ovens from rust; and for diminishing the friction of machinery.—As it is indistructible by heat, unless with the presence of air, it is used for making portable furnaces and crucibles.

IV. MINERAL CHARCOAL.

Mineral Charcoal is composed of various proportions of earth and iron, without bitumen. It has the fibrous texture of wood; black, and of a silky texture. It is found stratified in small quantities with coal. It is heavier than common charcoal; and is reduced to ashes before the blow-pipe, without smoke or flame. It soils strongly.

V. ANTHRACOLITE.

Anthracolite consists of carbon 72, silica

13.19, alumina 3.29, oxide of iron 3.47. It is dark iron-black; it burns without flame or odour. It connects coal with plumbago. Slaty Anthracolite or slaty glance-coal, is Welch *culm*, which is used extensively in the reduction of tin-ore. *Kilkenny coal* or *Blind coal*, which belongs to this class, is burnt in kilns for drying malt: the air which comes from it being free from fuliginous vapours.

Black chalk,—Black crayon, consists of silica 64, alumina 11, carbon 11; with a little water of crystallization and iron. It is bluish-black; soils the fingers; and is used in painting and drawing. Its streak is black.

VI. COAL.

Common *coal* when first kindled swells and exhales a kind of bitumen; thus the bitumen is separated from the carbon. It then burns with a red light. The separation is better effected in close vessels, the bitumen is melted out, and there are disengaged carbonate of ammonia, and carburetted hydrogen. The carbonaceous matter forms *coke*. The bitumen is used for vegetable tar or pitch; the coke for smelting, stoves, &c. and the gas for lighting streets, &c. *Bituminous shale*, or carbonaceous schist, is found in the neighbourhood of coal. It is composed of carbonated hydrogen gas, empyreumatic oil, carbon, silica, lime, &c. It frequently contains impressions of marsh and wood plants, and remains of shells. It contains particularly impressions of *adianthum nigrum* et *equisitum*, and species of fern. Two sides of a leaf are never represented in the same instance; and in the case of ferns, it is the impression of the inferior surface only of the leaf that is preserved.

Slate coal; Newcastle coal. It consists of carbon 75.28, hydrogen 4.18, azote 15.96. The common coal of England and Scotland are supposed by some writers to have been originally formed of a slaty clay impregnated with the vapours of petroleum, which were set at liberty by subterranean heat. The slate and cubical coal are used in private houses; the caking coal for smithy forges. The slate coal, from its keeping open, answers best for giving great heats in a wind furnace. The coal of South Wales contains less volatile matter than either the English or Scotch; hence, in equal weight, produces a double quantity of cast iron in smelting.

Cannel coal consists of carbon 64.72, hydrogen 21.56, azote 10.72. It burns with a bright flame, and flies into fragments. Its lustre is resinous; as it takes a fine polish, it is sometimes made into small boxes, &c. A pound of it will yield 5 cubit feet of gas equal in illuminating power to a mould candle of six in the pound. A gas jet which consumes half a cubic foot per hour affords light equal to the candle.

***

VII. JET.

Jet is generally velvet black. It is a little heavier than water; consists of carbon 75, bitumen 22, alumina 2. Its fracture is conchoidal. It burns with a greenish flame, and a bituminous odour. It is called, in Prussia, *Black amber*; there, and in the district of Aude, in France, it is cut into drinking vessels, snuff-boxes, mourning-bracelets, ear-rings, buttons, rosaries, &c.

VIII. BITUMINOUS WOOD.

Bituminous wood. Its principle constituent parts are vegetable earth 54, sulphate of iron 10.7, oxide of iron 12, with a small proportion of sulphur, sulphate of lime, and silica. It is generally of a brown colour. It occurs with common coal, and resembles the stems and branches of trees, a little flattened. It is like wood imperfectly charred: whole trees seem converted into it so as to resemble forests; in which the external shape of the branches and the annual rings of growth are observed. It is so light as nearly to float on water. It burns with a clear flame.

IX. NAPHTHA.

Naphtha is the lightest of all the dense fluids. It consists of carbon 87.21, hydrogen 12.79, and a little oxygen; even so little, that Sir H. Davy has employed it in preserving the new metals he has discovered. It is white, or yellowish; perfectly fluid and shining; and exhales an agreeable bituminous odour. It takes fire on the approach of flame. It dissolves resins, but is neither soluble in ether, or alcohol.

X. PETROLEUM.

Petroleum. It flows from coal-rocks and also from lime-stone; occurs in marshes and on the surface of spring-water. Its colour is yellow, brown, or greenish. It is semi-liquid.

and sometimes thicker. An oil is obtained from it by distillation similar to naphtha. It swims on water; inflames easily. It is composed of carbon, hydrogen, and a little oxygen. In Persia, Japan, Piedmont, &c. it is used in lamps for lighting streets and churches. It has been found in Treskirby mine, and in Huel Unity, Carharrack, and Huel Jewel.

XI. MINERAL PITCH. ELASTIC BITUMEN.

Elastic bitumen consists chiefly of bituminous oil, a little hydrogen gas, and charcoal. It is blackish brown. It has a strong bituminous smell. It removes the trace of plumbago, or black lead, like india rubber. It is about the weight of water. A variety of this, called *slaggy mineral-pitch*, said to contain the constituents in greater proportion, has been found in Carharrack mine.

XII. ASPHALTUM.

Asphaltum is derived from the name of the lake in Judea, where it is abundant, in a soft or liquid state. It consists of carbonated hydrogen, bituminous oil, carbon, silica, &c. It is brittle and breaks with a polish. It is black without transparency; melts easily and takes fire. It is slightly acted on by alcohol and ether. It has been considered as the principal ingredient in the Greek fire, so much employed in antient times. The mummies of Egypt are supposed to have been embalmed in it. The bricks of Babylon were cemented with hot bitumen. This mineral has been found, with yellow copper-ore, in Carharrack and Huel Unity mines.

XIII. FOSSIL COPAL. HIGHGATE RESIN.

Fossil copal is of a dull yellowish-brown. It occurs in irregular roundish pieces. It is semi-transparent; less frangible than common resin, and more so, than copal. When heated, at the flame of a candle, it gives out an aromatic odour; melts into a limpid fluid; and burns with a clear yellow flame.

XIV. RETINASPHALTUM.

Retinasphaltum is composed of resin 55, asphaltum 42, earth 3. Its colour is yellowish or reddish-brown, occurs massive, in crusts and angular pieces. The colour resinous, glistening ; brittle and translucent. It is elastic, but becomes hard when exposed to the air. On a hot iron it melts, smokes and burns with a bright flame, and fragrant odour. It is somewhat heavier than water. It has been found at Bovey Tracey, in Devonshire, in parallel layers adhering to coal.

XV. AMBER.

Amber is chiefly of a yellow, or orange colour. Its origin is involved in obscurity. It is found in nests among black charred forest trees deep under the earth, &c. hence, it is thought to be an indurated vegetable juice.— It is composed of carbon, hydrogen, and oxygen. It is translucent, and often contains leaves or insects. It is inodorous. Succinic acid is obtained from it by distillation. When rubbed it becomes strongly electrical. Electricity is derived from its Greek name *Electron.* Its solution in sulphuric acid is reddish-purple. No other acid dissolves it. From the fine polish it receives, its transparency and beauty, it is cut into bracelets, necklaces, cane-heads, snuff-boxes, &c. Before the discovery of the diamond and other precious stones, it was considered as the richest of jewels. One part of the oil obtained from distilled mineral pitch, and one and a half part of turpentine form a compound resembling amber, and which is frequently cut into ornaments and sold for it.

Tie up, in a fine muslin bag, the yolk of an egg, carefully freed from the white, and suspend it in a warm place. In about a month, it will acquire the appearance and some of the qualities of amber, becoming hard, transparent, electric, and capable of a fine polish.

XVI. MELLILITE.

Mellilite is of a honey-yellow colour; semitransparent; usually crystallized in small octahedrons, the angles often truncated. It refracts double. It is light, and softer than amber; becomes slightly electrical by friction. It consists of mellitic acid 46, alumina 16, water of crystallization 38. It is usually accompanied by sulphur. It burns without becoming sensibly charred, and leaves a white matter which effervesces slightly with acids. Amber, on burning coal, intumesces and spits, when its liquified particles drop and rebound, diffusing a fragrant odour; but mellilite becomes white without intumescence, or fragrance.

Amber, copal, and asphaltum, in a state of solution, in expressed or essential oils, or alcohol, are used as *varnish*. Before a resin is dissolved in a fixed oil it is necessary to render the oil drying. It is boiled with metallic oxides, when the mucilage of the oil combines

with the metal, while the oil itself unites with
the oxygen of the oxide. Oil of turpentine
accelerates the drying of the varnish. A solution of resin in oil of turpentine is the varnish
for paintings. The oil flies off and leaves the
resin.

K

EARTHY MINERALS.

The *earthy minerals* are ten, viz. the calcareous; the magnesian; the argillaceous; the silicious; the barytic; the strontitic; glucine; zircon; yttria; and thorina. They are all infusible before the flame of a common blow-pipe; but lime may be fused by the heat of a voltaic battery, or that of the oxy-hydrogen blow-pipe; and many of its combinations effervesce in acids. But the cause of that is very different from what produces the effervescence of metallic minerals. Metallic substances effervesce, from a part of the acid, or a part of the water, being decomposed, by the dissolving metal, which attracts to itself a part of their oxygen; and, when the oxygen is taken up by the metal, hydrogen gas is produced in the effervescence. That of lime-stone is produced by the separation of carbonic acid. Lime, combined with carbonic acid, and forming the basis of several other substances according to authors, constitutes a proportion of one-eighth of the crust of the globe. Sir H. Davy has discovered that it is an oxide of the metal *calcium*.

K 2

This is proved by the metal, during combustion, becoming by the absorption of oxygen, changed into the earth; and when the amalgam is thrown into water, hydrogen gas is disengaged, and the water becomes a solution of lime. Berzelius says, lime consists of calcium 72, and oxygen 28.

The *calcareous* minerals consist of lime combined with the *carbonic, phosphoric, fluoric, sulphuric, muriatic, nitric, boracic, arsenic*, and *tungstic*, acids; and with *silica*, forming

Carbonate
Phosphate
Fluate
Sulphate
Muriate
Nitrate ⎬ of lime.
Borate
Arseniate
Tungstate
Silicate

I. CARBONATE OF LIME.

Slate spar.—Specific gravity 2.5; its colour is white; greenish or reddish-white; massive; shining; pearly; feebly translucent. It is composed of lime 55, carbonic acid 41, oxide of manganese 3. It has been found in Polgooth mine.

Calcareous spar;—Crystallized carbonate of lime: spe. gr. 2.7;—consists of lime 56.4, carbonic acid 43.6. It is most generally distributed. It is crystallized in more than 600 different forms: the primary form of all is an obtuse rhomboid. The integrant particles have the same figure. Its colours are grey, yellow, red, green, and sometimes, blue. It is translucent. The most beautiful varieties are found in Derbyshire.

It has been found in the veins of the slate-quarries of Tintagel, with rock-crystal, chlorite, and adularia; and at Kynance-Cove, forming a vein in the serpentine, with a rhomboidal fracture;—at Padstow, in obtuse rhombs, of which the edges are truncated and bevelled :—in Polgooth mine, St. Austle ;—in six-sided prisms with flat tops, in Huel Buller ;—in three-sided prisms terminating in very oblique three-sided pyramids, and in six-sided prisms, the sides almost in an acute and triangular form, with the broad and narrow extremities alternating, and terminated in three-sided pyramids, resting on the acute planes of the prism, in the slate cliffs below Huel Owls and Huel Castle ;—in hexahedral tables; obtuse hexahedrons; and circular plates composed of minute crystals, sometimes much curved and finely aggregated, and often terminated at the circumference by six-sided prisms, with three-sided pyramids, crossing at right-angles, so as to produce the appearance of a broad wheel.

The hexahedral crystals are sometimes in-crusted with iron pyrites. Very large plates of it have been found at Cadgwith : some of these specimens have asbestous serpentine attached to them.

All the transparent varieties of calcareous spar have a double refracting power. *Iceland spar* is a pure carbonate; transparent, and shews the refracting power to great advantage.

Aphrite. It is nearly a pure carbonate of lime. It approaches to a silver-whiteness;

K 3

It occurs usually in a friable state; frequently massive; or in fine scaly particles. It soils:—is opaque. In acids it effervesces with violence, *spumam excitans*.

Agaric Mineral, or *Rock-Milk*. It is so called from its sometimes adhering to rocks like a fungus, *(agarium.)* It is also called *Lac Lunæ*, from the milky appearance it presents in a cave in Phrygia, formerly frequented by Diana. It is a pure carbonate of lime. It is composed of dusty particles without lustre, which weakly cohere. It nearly floats on water; stains much. It is used in Switzerland to whiten houses.

Chalk. Spe. gr. 2.3. It consists of lime 56, carbonic acid 43. Generally it contains a little silicious earth, and about 2 per cent. of clay: many specimens contain a little iron. Wherever found it is always the prevailing substance. Its hills have a smooth regularity of outline. The strata of most other substances are generally inclined to the horizon, but the direction of the chalk strata is almost always parallel with it.

Chalk, when purified by pounding and diffusion through water to separate silicious particles, forms *whiting*.

Chemists and starch-makers use it to dry their precipitates.

It is a marking material of mechanics. Moulds are cast in it:—it is used in the polishing of glass and metals; and with white of eggs or isinglass, as a cement.

When perfectly purified and mixed with vegetable colours, as litmus, turmeric, saffron, &c. it forms crayons for painting.

The *Vienna-white* is chalk purified to the highest degree.

A mixture of whiting and size in successive coats is laid on wood before it is gilded with gold.

In medicine, chalk is, in its purified state, used as an antacid.

Marble; spec. gr. 2.7. It consists of lime 56, carbonic acid 43, with a small quantity of water. It has purer colours, more transparency, and receives a higher polish, than compact lime-stone. *Parian marble* is snow-white. It hardens by exposure, which enables it to resist decomposition for ages. Works executed in it retain with the delicate softness of wax the mild lustre of their original polish. The finest Grecian sculpture is generally of Parian Marble. *Pentelic Marble,* from Mount Pentelicus, near Athens, when the arts had attained their full splendor, in the age of Pericles, was preferred to that of Paros. But sculpture in it has become decomposed, and exhibits an earthy surface, from the extraneous substances in the stone. The Parthenon was built of Pentelic Marble; and also the temple of Eleusis. *Carrara Marble*, on the eastern coast of Genoa, is milk-white. The *Florence Marble* is a compact marle inclining to compact lime-stone. It exhibits gothic castles, half destroyed; ruined walls; and old bastions; but when viewed nearer, these illusions vanish; and ruinous figures are converted into irregular marks which present nothing to the eye.

Lucullite; spec. gr. 3. It was so much esteemed by the Consul Lucullus, that he gave it his own name :—" *Primusq. ab Nili insulâ Romam invexit."* It is a carbonate impregnated with sulphuretted hydrogen, from which it derives a disagreeable odour, perceptible when rubbed.

The finest varieties of Britain are the black marbles in the district of Assynt, in Southerlandshire. It is distinguished by its deep black colour, its strong sulphureous smell when rubbed, and high specific gravity. It consists of lime 53, carbonic acid 41, with small proportions of black oxide of carbon, oxide of manganese, oxide of iron, silica, sulphur, potash, and combinations of muriatic and sulphuric acid.

One of the most remarkable of the English marbles is that of Anglesea, named *Mona marble*. It is greenish-black; leek-green; and sometimes purple; blended with white. The white part is lime-stone: the green shades are owing to serpentine and asbestus. The black marbles of England are varieties of Lucullite.

Madreporite. It is greenish-black. It is composed of lime 53, carbonic acid 41, with small proportions of the oxides of manganese, iron, and carbon, alumina, silica, &c. When rubbed, it emits a strong smell of sulphuretted hydrogen gas. It has been called *Anthraconite*, on account of the carbon it contains.

Compact, or *common lime-stone ;* spe. gr. 2.6. Its basis is carbonate of lime, but its composition varies, from the union of other substances; thus, its analysis is lime 53, carbonic acid 42, with small proportions of silica, alumina, iron, and water. It effervesces with acids without falling to pieces. Its colour is grey, or bluish. Petrefactions of animals and vegetables, especially the former, abound in it. There are also corals, shells, fishes, and sometimes amphibious animals.

Lime is found very sparingly in Cornwall.

In the parishes of Veryan and St. Michael Carhayes, the lime-rock appears in large masses on the surface of the soil; and has been advantageously employed as a manure. It was discovered by the *Rev. Jeremiah Trist*, in 1796.

It runs in strata of from two to three feet thick, north and south. A ton weight will produce nearly 20 single Winchester bushels of lime; to calcine which, are required four bushels and a half of culm. It forms a very hard cement for out-door work, something resembling Aberthaw lime; and, in respect of hardness and durability, it is evidently superior to common lime. This quality arises from its impurities; as the oxide of iron, with that of manganese, and some silica, are mixed with it. It does not contain magnesia. This rock resembles the lime rock of Padstow so nearly, as almost to be identical.

Aberthaw Lime-Stone, in Glamorganshire, is of a light blue or grey colour; this is owing to the presence of clay, which contains iron in a low state of oxidation. It forms a hard mortar under water, which is owing to the oxide of iron. As scales of iron from the forge are a good succedaneum for *Puzzolana*, (a species of porcelain earth containing iron, found on the heights of Puzzola, in Italy,) which is used for constructions under water, and becomes *" fortior quotidie."*

On the same principle, to resist the slanting rains so prevalent in Cornwall, very many of the houses are *pointed* with Aberthaw lime.

Magnesian lime-stone.—It is composed of carbonate of lime 51, carbonate of magnesia 44. It effervesces feebly with nitric acid :—this distinguishes it from common lime-stone.

When burnt, the magnesia is deprived of carbonic acid much sooner than the lime, because magnesia has a much weaker attraction for the acid than lime, and will remain in the caustic state for many months; and as long as it remains, the magnesia will not combine with carbonic acid, for lime instantly attracts carbonic acid from magnesia; and if there be not sufficient vegetable or animal matter to supply, by decomposition, carbonic acid to the soil, the magnesia impairs its fertility, and even poisons certain vegetables.—(See *serpentine.*)

Magnesian lime-stone is esteemed for cement; as it absorbs less carbonic acid from the atmosphere, it is less subject to decay than common lime. Yorkminster is built of this stone.

Miemite; discovered at Meimo, in Tuscany: *Magnesian spar;* spec. gr. 2.8.—It is asparagus-green; dissolves slowly in nitric acid. It is composed of carbonate of lime 53, carbonate of magnesia 42.5, with small proportions of carbonate of iron and manganese. It is translucent; massive; also crystallized in rhomboids; some of which are often truncated deeply on all their edges.

Pearl spar; Magnesian carbonate of lime; spec. gr. 2.5.—It is white; yellow;—occurs massive; and in obtuse rhomboids with curvilinear faces; and in flat and acute double three-sided pyramids, and rhomboids. It is easily broken into rhomboidal fragments. It consists of lime 43, carbonic acid and water 26, magnesia 10, oxide of iron 8, manganese 3. When the metallic carbonates increase, pearl spar passes into sparry iron-ore, or brown spar, which is a carbonate of iron:—(which see.)

Pearl.spar is distinguished from calcareous spar by its perfect pearly lustre, greater hardness, and higher specific gravity :—calcareous spar contains no magnesia. It occurred in Garras lead-mine, near Truro, in obtuse rhomboids—the primary form; it has also been found in Polgooth mine; in Huel Castle; and in a vein of calcareous spar in the cliff under Huel Owls; sometimes in transparent rhombs; at others, pearly and opaque; occasionally, botryoidal,—of a fine flesh-red, and white colour.

Marle ; spec. gr. 2.4; it is an impure carbonate of lime loosely aggregated. That which contains about 50 per cent. of chalk is compact, brittle, and is called *calcareous marle ;*—as thus analysed; carbonate of lime 50. silex 12, alumina 32, with a a small quantity of iron, or oxide of manganese. It effervesces with acids; burns to lime, and vitrifies with a strong heat. But if it lose 16 parts of carbonic acid from 100 by solution, in any acid, it is called *argillaceous marle ;*—it is earthy; of a grey colour; consists of dusty particles feebly cohering. It effervesces with acids, and emits an urineous smell when first dug. It is composed of carbonate of lime, alumina, silica, and bitumen. It is frequently called *Bituminous marle.* Fishes carbonized, or converted into coal are found in it, every one is in a contorted position, as if it had undergone a sudden death by the irruption of sulphureous, or metallic matter: it also contains petrified plants.

The only real marle in Cornwall, that is, such as contains a very large proportion of the carbonate of lime, has been found in the neighbourhood of the Veryan limeworks. A coral sand taken up in Carrick-Road, Falmouth Harbour; and above St. Mawes, is much used about Truro, and the adjoining parishes. It lies longer in the ground in an undissolved state than any other sand,—and it is said there are 82 kinds.—It effervesces strongly with acids; and its effects on the soil are both mechanical and chemical.*

The following analysis, by Mr. Michell, shews the composition of sea-sand which is extensively used as a manure:

Falmouth Harbour.

Carbonate of lime.,...........,...78.5	
Clay slate and silicious earth...21.5	
	100.0

St. Mawes.

Carbonate of lime..........,...55.0	
Clay slate and silicious earth...45.0	
	100

Helford.

Carbonate of lime...,.....,.....66.0	
Clay slate and silicious earth,..84.0	
	100

Perranzabuloe.

Carbonate of lime.............58.0	
Silicious sand..;...,..,.......47.0	
	100

Satin spar ; spec. gr. 2.7. It is composed of wavy parallel fibres, silky and translucent. Its constituent parts are lime 50.8, carbonic

* It is computed that the expense of land-carriage of sand, for the whole County, amounts to £30,000 per annum.—54,000 cart-loads of sand, are said to be carried, yearly, from Padstow alone. 4,000 horses have been laden with sand in one day.

acid 47.6. It is sometimes cut into crosses, necklaces, &c. in imitation of pearl.

Peastone. In the hot springs of Bohemia particles of quartz-sand rise with air-bubbles, and becoming incrustated with calcareous earth, from their weight fall down, and being agglutinated by stalactites they form peastone, which is a carbonate of lime slightly tinged of a yellowish white by oxide of iron. The globular concretions almost always contain in their centre the parent particle of quartz-sand; sometimes they are empty.

Stalactites;—Calc-sinter; spec. gr. 2.7. It is composed of lime 56, carbonic acid 48. The colour yellowish-white, green, &c. translucent. The red and green varieties, which are rare, owe their colour to metals. It is called *calcareous alabaster*, to distinguish it from *gypseous alabaster.*

Carbonate of lime is not soluble in water, unless that water itself be charged with carbonic acid; by this means stalactites is deposited from water loaded with carbonated lime in caverns, and suspended from vaults. The water, by its exposure to the air, loses that quantity of carbonic acid which promoted the solution of the lime: the water evaporates, and leaves the calcareous particles behind. Those flat, tabular, botryoidal masses formed on the floors of caverns, by water dropping, are called *stalagmites.*

Stalactites is the alabaster of antiquity, of which unguent boxes, and other small vessels, without handles, were constructed.

Vesuvian lime-stone. It is found of a blue colour among unaltered ejected minerals about Vesuvius. It seems to have been rolled. It contains 11 parts in 100 of water of compo-

sition: in common lime-stone there is none.
It is employed in mosaic work to represent
the sky.

Tuffaceous lime-stone. It is the most porous
and most impure of the carbonates of lime.
It seems to be the consequence of a process
similar to that by which stalactites is formed.
Waters producing this effect are called *petri-
fying* waters. They sometimes penetrate and
encrust vegetable and animal substances, and
convert them into stone. The articles placed
in the springs in Derbyshire, and which acquire the external appearance of petrifactions
are incrusted by calcareous tuffa.

Oölite; spec. gr. 2.6;—*Roe-stone.* It is so
called from its having once been supposed to
be petrified fish-eggs; or from its resemblance
to the *roe* of a fish. It is an impure carbonate
of lime, consisting of about 90 parts of calcareous, 10 of argillaceous earth, and iron. It is
soft when quarried, and hardens gradually in
the air.*

Arragonite: spec. gr. 2.9;—first found in
Arragon, in Spain. It is composed of lime 58,

* Newham quarry lies about half a mile south of Truro. Dr.
Thomson, (*Annals of Philosophy*, Oct. 1813, p. 256.) writes; "The
"town of Truro is built of a stone very much resembling Bath stone.
"It is a kind of *oölite*. I must conceive this quarry lies among the
"transition rocks, but as I did not see the quarry, I can give no in-
"formation respecting it." We beg leave to rectify the eminent
Professor's inadvertency.

1. Newham quarry is not oölite, but a species of horn-stone porphyry. There is only one house in Truro built of oölite, immediately
above the Miner's bank, the stones of which were brought by sea
from Bath. The walls built from Newham quarry become soon
covered with a dirty green, which is a *vegetable* incrustation:—in
summer, masons may be seen scraping it off, and the face of the stone
resumes its original fairness.

2. Calenick hill, on the west of the quarry, and over which the
high road passes from Truro to Falmouth is *primitive clay-slate*. The
Newham stone passes under this hill, and appears in the bed of the
stream above Calenick; hence, we cannot consider the rock in
which this stone is situated as *transition;* and its whole appearance
warrants this opinion.

carbonic acid 41. It is crystallized in regular six-sided prisms, longitudinally striated; and in fibres of a silky lustre diverging from a centre. The striæ, minutely inspected, appear longitudinal cracks extending down each lateral face. A fragment before the flame of candle splits into white particles. Fragments of calcareous spar, similarly placed, undergo no alteration. It is translucent, and refracts doubly. It contains strontites in a state of carbonate; a small quantity of which modifies the properties of the crystallization. It occurs in needle-form crystals, diverging, and forming botryoidal concretions, in Huel Edward, chiefly in small cavities in black and green crysocalla.

Calcareous stones when exposed to a strong heat are deprived of *carbonic* acid, and lose the property of effervescing, and become soluble in water. During this solution, they part with a quantity of absorbed heat; and thus, again, recover their affinity to carbonic acid, and their power of depriving other substances of it. Calcareous earth loses about 40 per cent. of weight, in burning, and becomes, from an inert substance, an acrid and active agent. If left upon a moist succulent part of animal or vegetable matter, it will corrode, dissolve, or weaken the cohesion of its parts. When water is poured upon it, it grows hot, smokes, splits, crumbles into pieces, and settles in a white powder. It is then *slacked* lime: and is now much heavier, by the water being united with it. A red heat will separate the water, and it will become quick lime again.

Quick lime, in the act of becoming mild,

prepares soluble, out of insoluble matter, and renders that nutritive which lay comparatively inert; hence, its efficacy in fertilizing soils, which abound in dry fibres, or inactive vegetable matter, by uniting with their carbon and oxygen, with which all vegetable substances abound.

Slaked lime mixed with sand, forms, with water, *mortar*, which in building is a cement superior to any other composition. The lime is the cause of the induration, partly from its combination with water, and partly by its absorbing carbonic acid from the air; hence, mortar gradually hardens into the state of carbonate. The sand prevents the cracking of the cement.

In one of the ground-apartments of St. Mawes Castle, facing the sea, the walls of which are 13 feet thick, an efflorescence * of a greyish white colour is produced in abundance. The walls are of granite. On the expanding left side of one of the windows it is particularly found: it falls down on the sole of the window, and may be formed into little heaps by the hand. The lime, when the Castle was built in the reign of Henry VIII. probably was made into mortar with sea water: the saline efflorescence is the result of the decomposition of common salt by means of the lime in the building; and, on analysis it is found to contain about two-thirds of the carbonate of soda, and one-third carbonate of lime. (See *alkaline salts.*)

Quick lime is used by the *soap-maker for*

* The water of crystallisation is that which enters into the formation of any salt; and such salts as fall to powder by exposure to the air, are said to effloresce, and the pulverulent substance is called *efflorescence.*

rendering its alkalies caustic by absorbing the
carbonic acid; by the *tanner*, for removing
the impurities of the skins; they are then
steeped in an infusion of oak-bark. This
consists of gallic acid and the tanning principle. By the former, the skins are deprived
of their oxygen; and the latter, combining
with the fibrous part of the skins, forms
leather.

Oxymuriatic acid gas is transmitted through
slaked lime, slightly humid; and a soft white
powder is formed, nearly inodorous, which,
when dissolved in water, affords a bleaching
powder.

Lime, though incapable of fusion when
alone, acts as a flux to other minerals. It
melts with borax; and combines so intimately with muriatic acid as to be insepa-
rable by heat alone. Fused with oxide of
iron it forms a black mass of a metallic appearance. With oxide of copper, a metallic
mass of red colour; with oxide of lead, a
yellow glass; with oxide of tin, a yellow glass;
with oxide of bismuth, a powder, or greenish
glass, according to the proportion of each
substance; with oxide of antimony, a semi-
transparent yellow mass; with zinc, a glass
of a deep yellow colour. These several combinations are so hard as to strike fire with
steel.

Lime water renders vegetable blues green;
the yellow, brown; and restores to reddened
litmus its natural purple. When left standing
in the air it attracts carbonic acid, and becomes an insoluble carbonate, while the water
remains pure.

Water containing carbonic acid is immediately rendered turbid by a few drops of lime-

water; because the carbonic acid, uniting with the lime, converts it into calcareous earth, which is not soluble in water.

A very minute quantity of lime in solution is easily discovered by dropping into it oxalate of ammonia;—a grain of lime dissolved in 43,000 parts of water is detected, by its forming an insoluble oxalate of lime in the form of a white powder.

Lime is used in medicine as an antacid, and an astringent.

II. PHOSPHATE OF LIME.

Apatite; spec. gr. 3.1. It is sometimes called *crystallized phosphate* of lime. It is composed of phosphate of lime 92, carbonic acid 6: according to Klaproth, lime 54.28, phosphoric acid 45.72. Its colour is green, of various shades, viz. yellow, blue, &c. It resembles the emerald, chrysolite, hyacinth, and other gems. It occurs crystallized in low three, or six-sided prisms, and in six-sided plates. Its primary crystal is a six-sided prism. It becomes electric by heat and friction; phosphoresces on coals, but does not decrepitate; and burns with a beautiful green light, which lasts a considerable time. It melts into a white enamel by the blow-pipe. It slightly effervesces with hot nitric acid, and forms sulphate of lime with the sulphuric, while its own acid is set at liberty. Whole mountains in Estremadura, in Spain, are composed of it. It is a dense stone, but not hard enough to strike fire with steel.

Apatite has been found in Stenna Gwyn, St. Stephens, in the granite of St. Michael's Mount; in Huel Kind, St. Agnes; and in

Godolphin Bal, in Breage parish. It occurs
of a yellowish-green colour, crystallized in
hexahedral prisms, in the rocks between Botallack and Huel Cock: and also of a greyish
white colour, united with hornblende, in the
cliffs of Huel Cock carn.

Phosphorite. Its constituent parts are lime
59, Phosphoric acid 34, with small proportions
of silica, fluoric, muriatic, and carbonic acids,
and oxide of iron. It is massive and not crystallized. The colour is yellowish, reddish,
and greenish-white; opaque. When rubbed
in an iron-mortar, or thrown on glowing coals,
it emits a green-coloured phosphoric light,
which it retains for some time after being
removed.

Asparagus-stone.—Conchoidal Apatite. It
is composed of lime 53, 32, phosphoric acid
45, 72. Its colour is bluish-green. It is always crystallized in equiangular six-sided
prisms, longitudinally striated. Translucent;
of splendent lustre, and approaching to soft.
It is soluble in nitric and muriatic acid, with
scarcely any effervescence. It does not phos-
phoresce when heated.

Lime is the basis of bones, and is found in
milk. Egg-shells, besides carbonate of lime,
contain phosphate. The interior of the shell
contains neither lime, nor phosphoric acid.
During incubation, therefore, the shell becomes thinner and thinner, till the embryo
has obtained a sufficiency for the formation of
its bones. Fowls kept from calcareous earth
lay eggs without shells. The rapid formation
of the bones of infants requires, that there be
be no waste of phosphate of lime; hence, their
urine contains none; while that of adults always contains that salt.

L 2

The farina of wheat contains phosphate of lime. The straw contains carbonate of lime and silica.

Phosphate of lime is difficult to fuse. Calcined, it forms a paste with water, used in making cupels. It is also used in polishing gems and metals; and for absorbing grease from cloth, or paper. The *burnt hartshorn* of the shops is a phosphate of lime.

III. FLUATE OF LIME.

Fluor spar; spec. gr. 3.1;—So named from its general use as a flux for the ores of iron and copper. It is composed of lime 67,75, fluoric acid 32.75. Two pieces rubbed together in the dark become luminous. When heated on glowing coals, it phosphoresces with a green light. It does not effervesce with acids like calcareous spar. The most beautiful varieties are found in Derbyshire; and there the ornamental articles of fluor spar are made.

The varieties of its crystals are numerous, of which the regular octahedron is the primary; producing the cube, rhomboidal dodecahedron, cubo-octahedron, octahedron with the edges replaced, cube with the edges replaced, yellow cubes with bevelled edges, bluish-green cubes with bevelled edges, the bevelling planes rough, and the primitive planes smooth; bluish-green cubes, edges slightly bevelled; dark-purple cubes, edges bevelled; light-green cubes, edges deeply bevelled; light-yellow cubes, edges very slightly bevelled; light-purple cubes, edges slightly bevelled. Massive green rhomboids, and cubo-octahedrons have been repeatedly found in Huel Unity and Huel Gorland. It occurs in the granite of St. Michael's Mount. It is sometimes incrusted with pyrites.

The most beautiful varieties of Cornwall have been found in St. Agnes. One of these consists of laminæ partly green and transparent, partly white and opaque.' At the time of writing, the author had before him one from that place, of a purple colour; crystallized in cubes, every plane or face exhibiting a flat four-sided pyramid, so as to form a solid, bounded by 24 triangular planes.

Chlorophane is a variety of fluor spar, consisting of lime and fluoric acid. Its colour is violet-blue. When placed on glowing coals, it throws out a beautiful emerald-green colour. It has been found in Pednandrae mine, Redruth.

The different colours of fluate of lime are owing to the different degrees of oxidizement of the iron and manganese they contain.

The human teeth contain fluoric acid, by which their durability is rendered greater than it would have been by phosphate of lime alone.

Concentrated sulphuric acid deprives fluor of its acid with effervescence.

Fluoric acid is employed in etching on glass, both in the gaseous state, and combined with water. It will pass by the quartz and mica of granite, and render the felspar muddy. It acts upon the onyx, agate, calchedony, flint, chrysopraze, opal, and Carrara marble.

IV. SULPHATE OF LIME.

Sulphate of lime :—*compact gypsum ;* spec. gr. 2.3. Its constituent parts are lime 32.7 sulphuric acid 46.3; water 21. Its primary form is said to be a rhomboidal dodecahedron. It is usually found in rhomboidal octahedrons; six-sided prisms with four summits; or lenticular. These crystals are often very transparent.

When exposed to heat, it loses its water of crystallization; decrepitates; becomes friable and white; and falls into powder. This is *plaster of Paris.*—It is called *gypseus alabaster* to distinguish it from *calcareous alabaster,* or stalactites.—It is one of the bases of stucco; used as a cement for making strong joints between stone; for joining tops or rims of metal to glass; for making moulds for the Staffordshire potteries; for cornices, mouldings, pillars, vases, chimney-pieces, busts, statues, &c. About 800 tons are raised annually in Derbyshire for these purposes.

Selenite. It includes all the crystallized specimens of sulphate of lime; and occurs in six-sided prisms, and oblique parallelopipeds. It is greyish, and yellowish white; transparent; and often refracts double. It yields readily to the nail. In Russia, where it abounds, it is used in several places as a substitute for glass in windows:—It has been used in the frostwork of the images of the Virgin Mary.

Chalk, when thrown into diluted sulphuric acid, though a violent effervescence is produced, is not dissolved, and it falls to the bottom, in a sediment considerably increased in bulk, because the compound produced by the sulphuric acid and the calcareous earth requires 500 times its weight of water to dissolve it. This sediment consisting of chalk and the salt which it has formed with the acid is sulphate of lime. A small proportion of this salt is a common impurity in spring water, and is the principal cause of the water being *hard*; because calcareous earth has a greater affinity for the sulphuric than for most other acids. When used with soap the sulphuric acid of the selenite unites with the alkali of the soap, and forms sulphate of soda, which remains in solution, while the lime unites with the tallow and forms an insoluble compound which will swim on water.

Anhydrite; spec. gr. 2.8. It contains no water of crystallization, which is the reason why it may easily be separated into fragments. It consists of lime 42, sulphuric acid about 57. It is harder and considerably heavier than gypsum; translucent; white; bluish; red. It is found in Tyrol crystallized in rectangular parallelopipeds, or octahedral and hexahedral prisms. *Vulpinite* is a variety of anhydrous gypsum: so called from Vulpino in Italy. It occurs massive; laminated; brittle. Its colour is grey; bluish. Composed of sulphate of lime 92, silex 8.

It takes a fine polish, and, as a marble, is used by the Italian statuaries.

Glauberite, another variety of anhydrous gypsum, is crystallized in an oblique four-sided prism, with a rhomboidal base, the terminal planes smooth, the 'lateral transversely striated: the crystals are of a light topaz yellow. It is composed of dry sulphate of soda 51, anhydrous sulphate of lime 49.

V. MURIATE OF LIME.

Muriate of lime;—Muriacite;—Cube spar; spec. gr. 2.5. It occurs in some salt mines. It consists of lime 40, sulphuric acid 55, and 1 of muriate of soda, or sea salt, by the pre-

sense of which it becomes glazed over with a
white friable enamel before the blow-pipe. It
does not exfoliate and melt like gypsum. Muriate of lime exists in nature, neither in much
abundance, nor in great purity.

VI. NITRATE OF LIME.

Nitrate of lime is composed of lime 32, nitric acid 57.44, water 10.56. It occurs in
fibrous efflorescences in caverns, or on calcareous rocks, in the neighbourhood of decayed
vegetable matter; in the mortar of old build-
ings, particularly those which have been exposed to animal effluvia. It diliquesces when
exposed to the air.

VII. BORATE OF LIME,

Dathotite; spec. gr. 3. It consists of lime
25, silica 36.5, boracic acid 24, water 4. It is
dull white; translucent; and very brittle. It
occurs in coarse concretions, which are easily
separable. It resembles prennite. The crystals occur in druses, and are small, flat, rectangular four-sided prisms. It fuses, with
intumescence, before the blow-pipe, into a
milk-white mass, and lastly into a rose-coloured
vitreous globule. At the flame of a candle it
becomes opaque, and may be pulverised by
the fingers.

VIII. ARSENIATE OF LIME.

Pharmacolite; spec. gr. 2.6. Its constituent parts are lime 25, arsenic acid 50.54;
water 24.46; its colour is white, and its surface is often tinged reddish by arseniate of

cobalt. It occurs in coarse small granular distinct concretions, or in delicate capillary crystals; it soils:—it is almost dissipated before the blow-pipe.

IX. TUNGSTATE OF LIME.

Tungstate of lime :—spec. gr. 6.6;—is composed of acid of tungsten 80.41; lime 19.40. It occurs crystallized in an acute octahedron, and in tetahedral pyramids. It is also amorphous; translucent; whitish-grey; yields easily to the knife. It resembles sulphate and carbonate of lead when massive; but it does not, like the latter, effervesce in acids.

It has been found in Pengelly-croft mine, Breage; in this ore the metal is combined with oxygen and calcareous spar. Tungstic acid has been found only in two minerals, viz. tungstate of lime, and tungstate of iron. (See *Tungsten.*)

X. SILICATE OF LIME.

Silicate of lime;—Tabular spar ;—spec. gr. 2.8. It consists of silica 50, lime 45, water 5. Colour, greyish-white; translucent; shines pearly; massive; and in angular-granular concretions. It effervesces in nitric acid for a moment, and then falls into grains. It is a rare mineral.

Botryolite,—a variety of Datholite,—is composed of lime 39.5, silica 36, boracic acid 18.5, water 6.5, oxide of iron 1. Its colour is white and yellowish-grey; its surface rough and dull; internally it displays a pearly lustre. It occurs botryoidal; semi-hard; translucent on the edges. It froths and melts before the blow-pipe into a white glass.

Idrocrase;—spec. gr. 3; composed of silica
85.50, alumina 33, lime 22.25, oxide of iron
7.50. It occurs abundantly in unaltered ejected
rocks in the neighbourhood of Vesuvius, crystallized in a quadrangular prism. It is considered a sub-species of pyramidal garnet:—
translucent, and of a yellowish, or brown-
green colour. It is harder than quartz; has
a double refraction; becomes electrical by
friction; and melts before the blow-pipe into
a yellowish, faintly-translucent, glass. At
Naples, it is cut into ring-stones.

MAGNESIAN MINERALS.

———

Magnesian minerals comprehend not only those in which magnesia is found in greatest proportion, but those also which it, though not the prevailing constituent, deprives of the hardness and lustre distinguishing silicious and argillaceous stones; and to which it imparts the unctuous and soft character, peculiar to the genus. Green of different shades is their general colour.

Magnesia, besides being found *native*, is combined with the *carbonic*, *sulphuric*. and *boracic*, acids; and with *silica*, and other matter, forming

Carbonate ⎫
Sulphate ⎬ *of Magnesia.*
Borate   ⎪
Silicate ⎭

1.—*Native Magnesia; Hydrate of Magnesia.* Spec. gr. **2.13.** It is composed of magnesia 70, water 30. It is laminated; and the laminæ are radiated; and it occurs also in regular hexahedral prisms. It is white, or tinged with green; sometimes transparent. It yields to the nail. It dissolves in diluted sulphuric, nitric, and muriatic acid, without effervescence. It has been found in serpentine.

Magnesia reddens turmeric, and renders the infusion of red cabbage, and the syrup of violets, green.—Used in medicine it is antacid, purgative, and lithontripic. The metallic base is called *magnesium.*

2.—*Carbonate of Magnesia;* —*Magnesite.* Spec. gr. 2.881. It consists of magnesia 46, carbonic acid 51, with traces of alumina, manganese, lime, and water. It is of a yellowish or grey colour, spotted with blackish brown. It has been found in serpentine. It is amorphous; soft; adheres to the tongue. When rubbed on a woollen cloth it becomes electric. It scratches carbonate of lime, and is scratched by fluate of lime. It effervesces in sulphuric acid, and yields on evaporation crystals of sulphate of magnesia.

Meerchaum;—*spuma maris.* Its constituent parts are silica 41, magnesia 18.25, lime 0.5, carbonic acid and water 39. It contains much water; hence, it is very hygrometric; it contains little carbonic acid; hence, it does not effervesce in acids. It is yellowish white; sometimes tinged with red; opaque; has an arid appearance; yields to the nail, adheres strongly to the tongue. It is nearly allied to magnesite. It is infusible before the blowpipe, but melts on the edges to a white enamel. When first dug it is unctuous and soft. It lathers water like soap, and is used by the Tartars for washing their hair, &c. It occurs in veins in serpentine in Cornwall.

Asbestus. It is composed of silica 64, carbonate of magnesia 17, carbonate of lime 13. It feels unctuous; occurs massive, and in capillary crystals at the Lizard; and in minute fibres in the slate rocks of St. Just: fine specimens occur in the prehnite vein between Botallack and Huel Cock, with nodules of prehnite imbedded in it.

Amianthus, or *Flexible Asbestus*. Its constituent parts differ very little from those of Asbestus. It is found in the serpentine at the Lizard, greenish-white or grey; blood-red; pearly; its fibres, white, green, reddish, are long, elastic, slender, and silky. Fine specimens have been found at the Frying-pan, Cadgewith. When rubbed it may be brought into a state resembling wool. Amianthus and asbestus differ as much as the finest unspun silk differs from compact fibrous wood. In amianthus the fibres are soft, fine, flexible and easily separated; in asbestus they are more closely compacted, harsh to the touch, and comparatively brittle: the lustre of amianthus is more silky; its colour lighter, and sometimes a silvery white. It was woven by the antients; and the dead were wrapped in it when placed on the funeral pile. Such cloth, when soiled, is restored to its primitive whiteness by fire. Schmeisser writes, " it is now used for making paper, and also for wicks."

Tremolite;—so called from Tremola, a valley in Switzerland. It is divided into three varieties by mineralogists; (that given among the silicates of magnesia, we consider a fourth;)—*Asbestiform Tremolite* is composed of silica 27, magnesia 18, lime 21, carbonic acid 26. It is of greyish, yellowish, or greenish-white. It occurs massive; and in capillary crystals. Its fracture is fibrous, and silky; lustre, pearly. It is soft and brittle;

when struck or gently rubbed in the dark it emits a pale reddish light: when pounded and thrown on coals, it gives a greenish light. It has been found in the rocks below Botallack, St. Just.—*Common Tremolite* consists of silica 50, magnesia 25, lime 18, carbonic acid and water 5. It is translucent; massive, in prismatic concretions; and crystallized in an oblique four-sided prism, truncated on the lateral edges; the lateral planes are longitudinally striated: the colour white, tinged with red. It melts with ebullition before the blowpipe into an opaque glass.—*Glassy Tremolite* consists of silica 35.5, magnesia 16.5, lime 26.5, carbonic acid and water 23. Its colour is white, frequently tinged with a slight red, blue, or green: it occurs massive in distinct concretions; and crystallized in long acicular shining prisms. The varieties of Tremolite melt with great difficulty before the blow-pipe. By a moderate heat, or gentle friction, they generally emit a luminous appearance: when scratched with a needle in the dark, they yield phosphorescent sparks. In all its varieties; in its fracture, whether by the hammer, or when the crystals are separated by the finger, it has a tendency to fibrous structure, often delicate, or flexible as acanthus. Tremolite is distinguished by its white colours; actinolite, by its light green; and hornblende, by its dark green.

Potstone;—Lapis ollaris;—composed of silica 39, magnesia 16, carbonic acid 20, oxide of iron 10, water 10. Its colour is greenish; occurs massive, and in granular concretions. From its softness it is easily formed into vessels, which, owing to its infusibility, are used for culinary purposes, in Egypt and Italy.

Lamps are made of it in Greenland and Norway, and ovens are lined with it.

3.—*Sulphate of Magnesia;*—It is composed of magnesia 19, sulphuric acid 33, water of crystallization 48. It is found efflorescing on brick walls and rocks. It crystallizes in quadrangular prisms. Its taste is cool and bitter. When the component parts of magnesian stones are not intimately blended, the magnesian earth, if pulverised, can be extracted by sulphuric acid, which is sulphate of magnesia. Sulphate of magnesia is known by the name of *Epsom salt,* one of the most valuable purgatives. It was furnished in considerable quantity by the mineral water of that place, and mixed with a portion of sulphate of soda. It is procured in greater abundance from the bittern, or liquor remaining after the crystallization of salt from sea water. Calcined magnesia dissolves in diluted sulphuric acid without effervescence:—and if magnesia, from the shops, be suspected to be adulterated with chalk, (which is sometimes the case,) a little diluted sulphuric acid will detect it, by forming with the magnesia a very soluble salt, whilst sulphate of lime remains insoluble.

4.—*Borate of Magnesia.*—Its constituent parts are boracic acid 68, lime 11, magnesia 13.5, with small proportions of alumina, silica, &c. Another analysis makes boracic acid 83.4, and magnesia 16.6:—Analysts differ much respecting this mineral. It is the only one of the magnesian genus in which the earth is found combined with an acid, and at the same time crystallized. The primary form of its crystals is the cube,—incomplete on its 12 edges, and at 4 of its solid angles:

the complete and incomplete angles being
diametrically opposite. The surfaces generally appear corroded. The perfect angles
exhibit negative electricity, and the truncated
angles, positive. The size of the crystals does
not exceed half an inch; generally they are
much less.—It is yellowish, greenish-white,
translucent; effervesces with acids; gives
sparks with steel.

5.—*Silicate of Magnesia*—consists of magnesia 54, silica 32.66, fluoric acid 4.08, potash
2.10, per-oxide of iron 2.83, water 1. It occurs
massive, the colour a wine or wax yellow;
translucent; scratches glass. Almost all the
magnesian silicates contain a combustible
substance which becomes charred when heated
in close vessels. If the mineral be then heated
in the open air, the charcoal burns away, and
the black colour appears. Steatite is a remarkable instance.

Steatite ;—Soapstone. Its constituent parts
are silica 45, magnesia 24.75, alumina 9.25,
potash 0.75, oxide of iron 1, water 18. It is
amorphous; white; grey; reddish-white;
green; unctuous; yields to the nail; translucent on the edges; soluble in acids slowly
without effervescence : It exhibits the same
colours as serpentine, but they are lighter.
In proportion as the colouring matter abounds
over the white, the steatite loses its distinctive
character, being neither so soft to the eye, nor
so unctuous to the touch; nor yielding to the
knife as the finer kinds. It writes readily on
glass. "Letters written with soap-stone upon
" glass, though insensibly fixed, are not re-
" moved by washing, but will always appear,
" when moistened by the breath."—*(Pryce)*
—It communicates positive electricity to seal-

ing-wax. It occurs in serpentine at the Lizard, where it is found passing into asbestus. From thence about 12 tons are exported annually to Swansea, for the manufacture of porcelain. The Earl of Falmouth receives a rent of £75. per annum, for the works. Steatite occurs of a greenish-white colour, and as unctuous as that of the Lizard, in Botallack, inclosing oxide of iron. It is found also in the tin-lode of Carnyorth Moor; and in small veins in slate, on the southern side of Pendeen Cove.

It was used by the antients to bleach linen; and by the Arabs instead of soap. A variety found in Arragon is used by artists under the name of *Spanish chalk*. Like fuller's earth, it extracts grease from silk and woollen. It is also employed in polishing gypsum, serpentine and marble. When pounded and slightly burned, it forms the basis of certain cosmetics.

Serpentine; spec. gr. 2.5.—It consists of magnesia 44, silica 44, alumina 2, oxide of iron 7.3, oxide of manganese 1.5, oxide of chrome 2. Its colour is green; greenish-black; straw-yellow; red. It feels somewhat unctuous; amorphous. It frequently contains magnetic iron-ore; so that mariners, off the Lizard, have often found the needle of the compass affected. The primary form of magnetic iron-ore,—the regular octahedron,—frequently occurs in it. Specimens of magnetic iron-ore from Norway, Sweden, Corsica, and New Holland, contain asbestus, steatite, jade, and magnesia. Serpentine is distinguished by a beautiful variety of colour; red is the most prevalent colour of the Lizard serpentine.

M

The serpentine district begins about half a mile from the Lizard light-houses. The whole of Goonhilly Downs consist of it. These are covered with an immense profusion of the *erica vagans*, one of the most beautiful flesh-coloured-blossom heaths. It defines the extent of the serpentine to the distance of 5 miles north. Not a single plant of it grows beyond the boundary of the serpentine; so essential and so congenial a magnesian soil appears to be for its existence.

On the sea shore, the serpentine is covered by a thin white crust, rifted in every direction. North east of the Lizard, the serpentine lies on green-stone.

About four miles south from Mullion, is Kynance cove, formed by a grand assemblage of dark serpentine rocks, beautifully polished by the attrition of the waves. About three miles further south is the soap-rock. The green-stone, north of Mullion, gradually passes into serpentine. Beyond Cadgwith the serpentine is of a dark green colour. The great mass of serpentine ends at Coverack cove, and is succeeded by an anomalous mixture of green and reddish-brown serpentine, compact felspar, saussurite, and diallage: for three miles a beautiful porphyry, having felspar for its base, extends to the Manacles. Green-stone interspersed with porphyry occurs at Porthoustacl, and a small bed of serpentine, on the south west of Porthallo, in the cliff, which rests on a talc rock of a reddish colour, lying upon argillaceous slate.

Magnesia in its mild state,—fully combined with carbonic acid,—as is the case in Goonhilly downs, in place of poisoning the soil, as it does when burnt, enriches it. There grows

a short grass of a deep green, which produces
excellent mutton; and the cultivated lands
bear crops of wheat equal to any in Cornwall.
(See *magnesian lime-stone.)*

In that tract is found precious serpentine.
Its colour is leek-green, or yellowish-green.
It is translucent. The fracture of common
serpentine is splintery, and fine grained; that
of precious serpentine is conchoidal.

Serpentine is cut in many places into various vessels, as cups, mortars, &c.

A species of rock which may be classed
among the serpentines is found on Clicka
Tor, about three miles north from Lis-
keard. The rock is of a dark bottle-green
colour, assuming that wavy and polished
exterior which characterises the magnesian
stones. The surface is sometimes en-
crusted with thin laminæ of precious serpentine of a green colour. And in the fissures
of the serpentine rocks is found actinolite, of a
leek-green. In the estate of Duporth, west of
Charlestown, St. Austle, in the cliffs of the
shore, serpentine is also found ;—and of a
greenish-white, in a range of rocks in a flat
field in the estate of Tregarthen, Gorran
parish.

Between the massive rocks on Clicka Tor, a
compact substance of a greyish-white colour,
consisting of crystalline spiculæ diverging
from centres, is found, which is *compact tremolite.* Crystals of the same mineral occur
about three-fourths of an inch in length, and
consist of thin tabular rectangular prisms. In
general their surface is dull, and they are of
a brownish ash-colour, resembling axinite.
Before the blow-pipe, a fragment of a crystal
melts into a greyish enamel. Its constituent

M 2

parts, according to Mr. Gregor's analysis, are

Silica.................62.2
Lime.................14.1
Magnesia............12,9
Oxide of iron........ 5.9
Water............... 1.

Oxide of iron is the cause of the different colours in the magnesian stones.

Schiller spar ;—spec. gr. 2.8; consists of silica 41, alumina 3, magnesia 29, oxide of iron 14, lime 1, water 10. It occurs of a brownish-green embedded in serpentine, in Coverack Cove, near St. Keverne. It is opaque; but translucent in thin folia, and yields to the knife. Its lustre semi-metallic; fracture, foliated. It is found inclosing angular pieces of felspar in the cliff below Huel Owls.

Diallage ;—Smaragdite ;—spec. gr. 3.1; is composed of silica 50, magnesia 6, alumina 11, lime 13, oxide of iron 5.3, oxide of copper 1.5, oxide of chrome 7.5. Its colour is generally grass-green, with a silky lustre; translucent :—it occurs massive in the serpentine district, particularly at Coverack Cove. It is cut into snuff-boxes, ear-rings, and a variety of other ornamental articles.

Chlorite ;—spec. gr. 2.6; its constituent parts are silica 26, alumina 18.5, oxide of iron 43, magnesia 8, muriate of soda 2. Its colour is generally a dark-green. It is with difficulty fusible *per se.* It discovers a little clay smell when breathed on. It is called *peach* in Cornwall. It frequently accompanies the oxide of tin and mispickel, and is disseminated through the same matrix in small shining earthy grains or spangles, which fall to powder by the pressure of the fingers.

Earthy chlorite, of green, glimmering scales, forms the vein-stone of several of the lodes in St. Just. It is also one of the constituents of the rocks at Chycornish Carn; it is composed of silica 50, alumina 26, lime 1.5, oxide of iron 5, potash 17.5.

Green earth;—spec. gr. 2.6; composed of silica 53, oxide of iron 28, potash 10, magnesia 2, water 6. It is very soft; the lustre of its streak is glistening. It often incrustates the agate balls found in amygdaloid; and in this state it is similar to chlorite. It is the " Mountain-green" of artists in water-colours. The colour is not so lively as that from copper, but it is more durable, as it is not altered by acids. When slightly burnt it affords a rich brown.

Talc;—spec. gr. 2.7; it is white; light-green; blue; frequently tinged with a shade of yellow; splendent; translucent; soft.—Composed of silica 62, magnesia 27, alumina 1.5, oxide of iron 3.5, water 6. It does not effervesce in acids. It is distinguished from mica by being not so elastic. It occurs compact and whitish-green at the Lizard, Kynance cove, and Porthallo; massive, composed of aggregated crystals in Stenna Gwyn mine, St. Stephens; in six-sided tables, in Gwennap; and in laminæ in the upper lode of Huel Cock, St. Just.

The Romans prepared a beautiful blue, or purple colour, by combining talc with the colouring fluid of particular kinds of testaceous animals, viz.: *buccinum reticulatum, et buccinum lapillus*, which abound on the shores of the Mediterranean. With carmine and benzoin, it is used in *rouge :* this cosmetic communicates a peculiar softness to the skin without injury. Gypsum figures receive their flesh colour, by being rubbed with talc.

m 3

Talc-slate—occurs in serpentine, massive, at the Lizard; greenish-grey; soft and unctuous, but possessing less lustre than the above. It becomes hard in the fire, and is made into various vessels for boiling, &c.—It is used for drawing lines by carpenters, tailors, hatmakers, and glaziers: the lines are not so easily effaced as those of chalk; and remain unaltered under water.

Mountain-cork—is composed of silica 56, magnesia 26.1, lime 12.7, alumina 2, oxide of iron 8. It is yellowish; greyish-white; ash-grey; very soft; emits a grating sound when handled; sometimes elastic like common cork, and has like it a meagre feel; swims on water; melts with great difficulty. It is found in serpentine, generally in flat pieces. It occurs in conjunction with axinite in Roscommon cliff, St. Just. When in thinner pieces and of a closer texture, it is called *mountain leather*.

As it contains no carbonic acid, it cannot be properly called a variety of asbestus, though it resembles it: they are distinguished; asbestus generally exhibits even or parallel fibres; in mountain-cork they are short and interwoven, and of an interlaced texture.

Actinolite; of this there are three varieties. *Asbestiform actinolite;* spec. gr. 2.7; greenish; grey; massive; fibrous; it melts before the blow-pipe into an opaque brown glass.— It has been found at Duporth, St. Austle; and in the rocks near St. Michael's Mount. It occurs in Huel Unity; massive; composed of a congeries of elastic capillary crystals, easily crumbled between the fingers; the crystals themselves, hexahedral prisms, are hard. It occurs also in small veins in the slate and hornblende rocks, near Cape Cornwall; and in Botallack cliffs, resembling a mass of compressed crystals, of a bottle-green, and deep-brown colour; it also occurs in the slate cliffs below Huel Owls, St. Just. Its component parts are silica 47, lime 11.3, magnesia 7.3, oxide of iron 20, oxide of manganese 10.— 28.2 of alumina and 3.84 of tungstic acid have been found in 100 parts of asbestiform actino-lite of Cornwall.

Common actinolite; spec. gr. 3.0;—is leek-green; occurs massive, and crystallized; the crystals longitudinally striated, diverging, of an external vitreous lustre. It melts by the blow-pipe into a black scoria. It has been found at Dartmoor, Devon.

Glassy actinolite; spec. gr. 3.1; its constituent parts are silica 50, magnesia 19.25, lime 9.75, oxide of iron 11, alumina 0.75, oxide of manganese 0.5, oxide of chromium 3, potash 0.5. It is translucent; lustre, vitreous; pearly; green. It has been found massive and in acicular crystals in Huel Unity. It melts by the blow-pipe into a glass.

Hyperstene ;—called also *Labrador Horn-blende,* because first found on the coast of La-brador. Spec. gr. 3.4. It consists of silica 54.25, magnesia 14, oxide of iron 24.5, alu-mina 2.25, lime 1.50, water 1, and a trace of manganese. It is greenish-black, or brown. When fractured it exhibits a metallic lustre. It is found in opaque rolled pieces. Infusible *per se.* It occurs massive at Coverack Cove, Lizard. When polished into brooches or ring-stones, it displays a beautiful copper-red colour.

Bronzite ;—spec. gr. 3.2; consists of silica 60, magnesia 27.5, oxide of iron 10.5, water 0.5,

It is brown, of a pseudo-metallic lustre, resembling that of bronze. It is found massive, and lamellar: calcareous spar is frequently between the laminæ. The thin plates are transparent.

Anthophillite; spec. gr. 3.2;—its colours resemble those of the flower anthophyllum. It occurs massive, and crystallized in flat six-sided transparent prisms, longitudinally striated. Its constituent parts are silica 56, alumina 13.3, magnesia 14, lime 3.33, oxide of iron 6, oxide of manganese 3. It is brownish and splendent. With borax before the blow-pipe it melts with difficulty into a grass-green transparent bead.

Nephrite; spec. gr. 3. Its constituent parts are silica 50.5, magnesia 31, alumina 10, oxide of iron 5.5, water 2.75, oxide of chromium 0.05.* It is green, or greenish-white; translucent; feels unctuous; occurs massive. It is nearly allied to serpentine. It is valued as an ornamental stone: artists engrave figures upon it: in Turkey it is cut into handles for military weapons. It was formerly used in preventing, or alleviating, *nephritic* complaints; hence, its name.

Axe-stone is a variety of nephrite: it is used in New Zealand, and other south sea islands, for hatchets, &c. Some small specimens of it have been found in the Lizard serpentine district.

Chrysolite;—spec. gr. 3.5, is composed of silica 39, magnesia 43.5, oxide of iron 19. It is crystallized in eight-sided prisms termi-

---

* *Saussure* excludes nephrite from the magnesian stones; his analysis is—silica 58.75, lime 12.75, alumina 1.5, oxide of iron 5, oxide of manganese 2, soda 10.75, potash 8.5, water 2.25. *Phillips* prefers this:—that in the text is *Vauquelin's* analysis, which the greater number of authors we have consulted follow.

nated by a pyramidal summit, truncated at the apex. The lateral planes are longitudinally striated. Its primary form is a right prism with a rectangular base. It has a double refraction. The colour is pistachio-green, sometimes shaded with a golden yellow. It fuses with borax into a pale green glass.

It is employed in jewellery as a precious stone :—as it is the least hard of the gems, if not carefully kept, it becomes dull by wearing.

Olivine ;—spec. gr. 3.24 ; it is a variety of prismatic chrysolite. Olive-green ; occurs massive; sometimes crystallized in rectangular four-sided prisms; of a shining lustre; translucent; melts with borax before the blow-pipe into a dark-green bead. It is composed of silica 50, magnesia 38.5, oxide of iron 12, and a trace of lime. It loses its colouring matter (oxide of iron) in nitric acid.

Augite : Pyroxene ; spec. gr. 3.6 ; composed of silica 52, magnesia 10, lime 13, oxide of iron 14, with small proportions of alumina and manganese. It generally occurs among volcanic rocks supposed to have existed prior to the eruption, in small six or eight-sided prisms; colour green, or brownish-black ; translucent.

Diopside, a variety of augite, spec. gr. 3.3 ; is greenish-white ; translucent ;—it consists of silica 57.5, magnesia 18.25, lime 16.5, oxides of iron and manganese 6. It occurs massive; and crystallized in oblique four-sided prisms, which are sometimes truncated on the acute lateral edges ; bevelled on the obtuse, and the edge of the bevelment truncated. Sometimes it is found crystallized in eight-sided prisms, the narrow lateral planes smooth; and the broad longitudinally striated.

Sahlite. Spec. gr. 3.22. It is named from the silver mine of Sahla in Portugal, where it was first found. It is composed of silica 53, magnesia 19, lime 20, alumina 3, oxide of iron and manganese 4. Its colour is greenish grey; occurs massive in lamellar concretions; and crystallized in a tabular rectangular four-sided prism. Translucent on the edges.

Coccolite; spec. gr. 3.3; consists of silica 50, lime 24, magnesia 10, alumina 1.5, oxide of iron 7, oxide of manganese 3. It occurs massive in various shades of green; and crystallized in six-sided prisms, which are generally rounded on the angles.

ARGILLACEOUS MINERALS.

Colour, the most variable and fallacious of all the external characters, had allied argilla-ceous minerals with those of the silicious genus; but chemical analysis proves them to be distinct, and they are now free from the perplexity of mineralogical discussion. Alu-mina is their base; and in them it is the pre-dominating ingredient.

Alumina, from its constituting the plastic principle of all clays, was formerly called ar-gillaceous earth; and it was deemed primitive matter, until Sir H. Davy discovered that it is a metallic oxide;—and the metal which it contains he has named *aluminum*.

Alumina is found combined with the *sul-phuric, fluoric, phosphoric*, and *chromic*, acids; and united, chemically or mechanically, with *silica*, forming

Sulphate
Fluate
Phosphate } of *Alumina.*
Chromate
Silicate

1.—*Sulphate of alumina;—Alum.* It is composed of alumina 10.86, sulphuric acid 34.33, water 45, potash 9.81. According to another analysis, alumina 15.25, sulphuric acid 77, oxide of iron 7.50, potash 25. Colour snow-white; opaque; soft.

It is produced but in small quantities in nature : it generally occurs as an efflorescence on argillaceous minerals, crystallized in capillary octahedrons. It is chiefly manufactured from laminated stony matter similar to, but softer than, slate.

Alum, at a moderate heat, fuses and froths till its water of crystallization be evaporated, at which period it has the form of a white friable substance, called calcined alum, which retains the greatest part of its acid, when not too much heated.

Alum is employed as a mordant in dyeing : it opens and cleans the pores on the surface, and renders the substance fit for receiving colours; and, as it becomes decomposed, the colour becomes fixed.

Printers' cushions, and the blocks used in the calico manufactory, are rubbed with burnt alum to remove any greasiness.

It is used in tanning; and in making pyrophorus.

Paper impregnated with it excludes moisture; hence, its use in keeping gunpowder :— such paper is employed in silvering brass, without heat; and in whitening silver.

Alum, in milk, accelerates the separation of butter.—When added to tallow, it renders it harder.—It increases the tenacity of ferinaceous pastes. It is sometimes mixed with flour to make the bread whiter. It renders turbid water limpid, without any bad quality.—

Alum may be decomposed by the alkalies,
fixed, or volatile, because of their greater
affinity for sulphuric acid than for alumina.
If, therefore, the smallest quantity of alum
be dissolved in water, a few drops of any
alkaline solution will precipitate the alumina. A solution of chalk or of silver in
the nitric acid is rendered turbid by a solution of alum in water. Crayons consist
generally of tinged alum earth. Almost all vegetable colouring matter may be precipitated
into lakes more or less beautiful by means of
alum. In medicine it is employed as an astringent.

Automalite. Its constituent parts are alumina 42, silica 4, oxide of zinc 28, oxide of
iron 5, sulphur 17. Occurs in regular octahedrons, small, foliated longitudinally. Colour,
a muddy blue, inclining to mountain-green;
dark green; opaque; fuses with borax. It
belongs to the ruby genus.

2.—*Fluate of Alumina; Topaz;* spec. gr.
3.5; the constituent parts of the Brazilian
topaz are alumina 50, silica 29, fluoric acid
19;—of the Saxon topaz, alumina 57.45, silica
34.24, fluoric acid 7.75. Its primary crystal
is a rhombic prism: the lateral planes longitudinally striated; the accuminating planes
smooth. The rhomboidal base of its crystals
and longitudinal striæ distinguish the topaz
from other minerals. The topaz consists of
four-sided crystals; those of quartz are six-
sided; and the striæ on the quartz are horizontal. The colour of topaz is wine yellow,
in every degree; nearly transparent; splendent; refracts double: the oriental topaz is
orange-yellow.

Topaz is found in nests in transition clay-slate; with phosphate and carbonate of lime and tin-stone in Huel Kind, St. Agnes; and with tin-stone, felspar, and apatite, at St. Michael's Mount. The Cornish topazes are small; sometimes white; sometimes yellow.

Mr. Gregor* detected *potash* in the Brasilian, Cornish, and Scotch topazes. *Cairngoram*-stone, or Scotch topaz, which is a yellow-coloured rock-crystal, when well-cut, resembles real topaz.

Schorlite; spec. gr. 3.53; composed of alumina 48, silica 34, fluoric acid 17, with a trace of iron and manganese:—occurs massive, and in long hexahedral prisms longitudinally striated, sometimes truncated on the terminal edges and angles. It is composed of thin parallel prismatic concretions. Colour straw-yellow; dull reddish-white; translucent; has a general resemblance to schorl; allied to topaz; melts with borax into a transparent glass.

Cryolite; spec. gr. 2.95; composed of alumina 24, soda 36, fluoric acid and water 40:— Colour greyish-white; occasionally brown from an admixture of iron; of a lamellar structure; transparent, and becomes more so in water; lustre inclining to pearly; crystallized in octahedrons. It dissolves in sulphuric acid, fluoric acid gas being disengaged; not so hard as fluor spar; melts before the flame of candle; before the blow-pipe fuses into a transparent globule, which becomes opaque on cooling.

3.—*Phosphate of Alumina; Wavellite;*— spec. gr. 2.5; first found at Barnstaple, Devon-

* *Annals of philosophy,* vol 8, p. 276.

shire, by Dr. Wavell. It's constituent parts are, according to Berzelius,

Alumina	35.35.
Phosphoric acid	33.40.
Fluoric acid	2.06.
Lime	.50.
Oxide of iron and manganese	1.25.
Water	27.*

It is also called *Hydrargillite*, from the great proportion of water in its composition: —occurs in protuberances, white or greenish; radiated and of a pearly lustre; of a stellated diverging fracture.

Some specimens are botryoidal, stalatitic, and crystallized. Of two lying before the author, one is on a cuneiform fragment of slate clay. It is covered with asterisms; the centres raised; the pearly radii declining to the circumference: from one corner of the matrix one stella shoots forth diverging radii, amidst which another lies, and gives them a diagonal direction. The other specimen consists of stellæ, studded over the surface of the bluish slate clay;—at the ends of the stone the wavellite asterisms appear in the fracture.

Two varieties in veins accompanying fluor spar, tinstone and copper pyrites, in granite, have been found at Stenna Gwyn, St. Stephens; 1.—*Soft wavellite*, an assemblage of minute crystals attached to tufts of quartz radiating sometimes like a fine powder of down; colour, white; 2.—*Compact wavellite*, an assemblage of crystals, like mamillary protuberances, size of small peas, striating from a centre.

* Dr. Ure, in his chemical dictionary, (article *Alumina*,) says, " Wavellite, a beautiful mineral, consists almost entirely of alumina, " with about 28 per cent. of water."

Mr. Gregor's analysis of Cornish wavellite is

    Alumnia.................58.70
    Oxide of iron........... 0.19
    Lime................... 0.37
    Silica 6.12
    Water.................30.75.

By the aid of heat it is soluble in mineral acids.

4.—*Chromate of Alumina; Spinelle*; spec. gr. 3.6; composed of alumina 84.47, magnesia 8.78, chromic acid 6.18. Its primary crystal is the regular octahedron; it occurs also in tetrahedrons:—colour, red, blue, green, yellow; splendent, and of a vitreous lustre. The scarlet variety is the Spinelle ruby; the cochineal red, the Balais ruby; the orange red, the Rubicelle ruby; the violet coloured, the Almadine ruby.

5.—*Silicate of Alumina; Corundum;*— specific gr. 4; is composed of alumina 90, silica 7, oxide of iron 1; colour, greenish, and white of various shades; azure-blue, and peach blossom-red; massive; surface, rough. Specimens from the parish of Madron, Cornwall, are reddish-brown and massive. Its hardness is inferior to that of the diamond, but superior to that of other minerals: from its aggregation it is scarcely acted on by chemical agents.

It is used for cutting and polishing hard minerals.

Adamantine spar, a subspecies of corundum and less pure; occurs crystallized in a hexahedral prism with a three-sided or six-sided pyramid; has a greenish, and sometimes a reddish tint. With borax before the blowpipe, it fuses into a colourless glass.

Sapphire;—spec. gr. 4; consists of alumina

90.5, silica 5.25, oxide of iron 1 :—crystallized in small hexahedral prisms with six-sided pyramids, the planes transversely striated; sometimes the prism is four-sided. When translucent it exhibits a six-rayed opalescence; frequently shews two, sometimes three colours on the same crystal:—Its colour is blue of various shades, red, white, yellowish-green. It refracts double.

The crimson and carmine red, are the oriental ruby of the jeweller. The blue is next in value. The white varieties almost rival the diamond in lustre.

It is cut with diamond powder, and polished with emery. With borax by the blow-pipe it melts slowly into a colourless glass.

Ceylanite; spec. gr. 3.77; so called, because first found in Ceylon, consists of alumina 72.25, magnesia 14.64, protoxide of iron 4.26, silica 5.48;—occurs in rolled pieces; and frequently crystallized in a regular octahedron; more commonly the edges are truncated, and small facets are in their places. Colour indigo-blue; passing into a faint green: has a rough surface with little external lustre. Before the blow-pipe it melts into a green glass.

Emery;—spec. gr. 3.68; is composed of alumina 86.5, silica 3, oxide of iron 4. Colour a bluish-grey; lustre, adamantine; it is so hard as to scratch topaz.

Its powder is used with oil for polishing metals; and with water for polishing hard stones: when triturated it is diffused in water, which is allowed to settle a longer or shorter time, according as fine or coarse powder is required,—the finest is obtained by elutriation.

Pyrophysalite;—spec. gr. 3.45; interme-

N

diate between topaz and schorlite:—composed of alumina 53.2, silica 32.2, lime 0.8, oxide of iron 0.8;—colour mountain-green. The powder effervesces slightly in acids when heated.

Chrysoberyl ; spec. gr. 3.76; its constituent parts are alumina 71.5, silica 18, lime 6, oxide of iron 1.5; occurs in angular or rolled pieces, not much larger than a pea, and crystallized in eight-sided prisms terminated by six-sided pyramids; the pyramids sometimes present 28 facettes :—colour asparagus-green, passing into various shades, often exhibiting a milk-white opalescence ; translucent; possesses double refraction; becomes electric by friction. It is a rare gem of the second order.

Cyanite ; spec. gr. 3.5; its constituent parts are alumina 55.5, silica 38.5, oxide of iron 2.7, lime 0.5, water 0.7; its principal colour is sky-blue ;—also white ; grey ; occurs massive, and crystallized in oblique flat tetrahedral prisms. The massive varieties translucent; the crystals generally transparent; some of which, by friction, acquire negative; others, positive electricity ; from these double powers, it is called *Disthene.* It fuses by the blow-pipe with borax into a colourless glass.

Fibrolite ;—spec. gr. 3.75; consists of alumina 58.2, silica 38, oxide of iron and loss 3.7; colour white; grey ; harder than quartz: occurs usually in fragments, shapeless, fibrous and traversed by cracks.

Pinite ; spec. gr. 2.95; so called from the Pini gallery in the mines of Schneeberg, in Saxony, where it was first found. It occurs massive, and in equiangular six-sided prisms, and, from truncation of the lateral edges, in twelve-sided prisms. Its constituents are alumina 63.75, silica 29.5, oxide of iron 6.75; colour blackish-grey; brown; red; opaque; feels unctuous. It is imbedded in the granite of St. Michael's Mount. It has been confounded with mica, but it never inclines to the tabular form. It is allied to schorl.

It occurs also in the granite rocks on the hills south east of Trewellard, crystallized in six-sided prisms.

Kollyrite—consists of alumina 45, silica 14, water 42; soft; light, and unctuous; soils slightly. Occurs as a wet tenacious white clay, from which the water is separated very slowly. When desiccated, it becomes like starch : it absorbs water with a hissing noise. Infusible ; dissolves without effervescence in nitric acid.

Nepheline ;—spec. gr. 2.6 ; translucent pieces, when immersed in nitric acid, become cloudy in the interior :—called also *Somnite,* from the mountain Somna, in Naples, where it is found in drusy cavities. Its constituents are alumina 49, silica 46, lime 2, oxide of iron 1. Occurs massive, and crystallized in six-sided prisms, and in a thick-sided table ; the lateral edges truncated ; the primary form a rhomboid ;—colour white ; resembles phosphate of lime, but does not, like it, give a phosphorescent light when placed on glowing coals.

Andalusite ;—spec. gr. 3.16 ; first found in Andalusia, in Spain;—consists of alumina 52, silica 32, potash 8, oxide of iron 2; occurs massive of a flesh, sometimes of a rose-red, colour ; and crystallized in rectangular four-sided prisms ; translucent. It has been found in Dartmoor, Devonshire.

Lazulite ; Lapis Lazuli ; azure stone ;— spec. gr. 2.85; it is composed of alumina

N 2

14.5, silica 46, lime 28, oxide of iron 3, sulphate of lime 6.5, water 2. Colour, a rich azure blue; chemists differ as to the ingredients; some analyse it thus,—silica 34, alumina 33, sulphur 3, soda 22. Occurs massive; lustre glimmering; opaque; intumesces in a strong heat, and melts into a yellowish-black mass.

Ultramarine; a beautiful and unchangeable blue, is prepared from this mineral:—the extraction of the paint is considered as a species of saponification. The specimens from Persia, China, and Great Bucharia, are made red hot, and thrown into water to render them pulverisable:—the powder is combined with a varnish of resin, wax, and boiled in linseed oil; this is kneaded in a linen cloth with hot water; the second water gives a blue of the first quality. The process is founded on the property which the colouring matter has of adhering more firmly to the foreign matter than to the resinous paste.

Azure stone is used in mosaic work; it is supposed by some that the sulphur in it exists in the state of sulphuret of iron, which is the cause of its colour. It is deprived of its colour by all the mineral acids. It melts before the blow-pipe into a white enamel.

Azurite—so called from its resemblance to azure-stone. It occurs granular, and more generally found crystallized in quadrangular prisms of an indigo-blue colour, in a gangue of quartz. Its constituents are alumina 60, silica 10, magnesia 18, oxide of iron 2.5, lime 2. Opaque; nearly as hard as quartz; softer than azure-stone. With borax it forms by the blow-pipe a clear pale yellow pearl.

Staurodite; prismatic garnet;—spec. gr.

3.5; it is composed of alumina 44, silica 33, lime 3.84, oxide of iron 13, oxide of manganese 1. It is crystallized in two sided prisms, which intersect each other at right angles, or obliquely; hence, it sometimes called *cross-stone;* colour, a dark reddish brown, splendent, opaque, sometimes translucent; precious garnet, which it in some respects resembles, is mixed with blue.

Staurodite is brown. Precious garnet occurs in grains; staurodite is crystallized. Precious garnet is fusible, staurodite is not.

Alumina is widely diffused in nature. It forms a proportion of every rock, and every soil. It is the basis of bricks, pottery, and porcelain. Its combinations constitute fullers' earth, ochres, pipe-clay, &c. Its affinity for vegetable colours makes it useful in the preparation of lake, and in dyeing, and calico-printing.

SILICIOUS MINERALS.

Silica is one of the most abundant substances in nature. It forms a constituent part of about two-thirds of all the earthy minerals, whose composition is known. It has been discovered by Sir H. Davy to be a compound of a peculiar combustible principle with oxygen. By passing the vapour of potassium over silica in an ignited tube, he obtained a dark powder, containing the metal *silicium*, the basis of the earth.

As silica has the power of neuteralizing the alkaline earths, as well as the common metallic oxides, some authors would have it ranked among acids in many minerals.

We divide the silicious minerals into two classes; those containing silica in a proportion of not more than 60 per cent. we call *pro-silicious*; and those, whose proportion of silica is above 60 per cent. we term *per-silicious*.

1. *Mica,*
2. *Lepidolite,*
3. *Hornblende,*
4. *Indianite,*
5. *Basalt,*
6. *Wacké,*
7. *Clink-stone,*
8. *Clay-slate,*
9. *Porcelain clay,*
10. *Bole,*
11. *Lithomarge,*
12. *Fuller's earth,*
13. *Meionite,*
14. *Chiastolite,*
15. *Saussurite,*
16. *Agalmatolite,*
17. *Scapolite,*
18. *Elaolite,*
19. *Lythrodes,*
20. *Zeolite,*
21. *Laumonite,*
22. *Mesotype,*

23. *Stilbite,*
24. *Apophyllite,*
25. *Chabasite,*
26. *Analcime,*
27. *Natrolite,*
28. *Prehnite,*
29. *Garnet,*
30. *Allochroite,*
31. *Sodalite,*
32. *Pyrope,*
33. *Haüyne,*
34. *Melanite,*
35. *Cinnamon-stone,*
36. *Leucite,*
37. *Tourmaline.*
38. *Schorl.*
39. *Epidote,*
40. *Zoisite,*
41. *Axinite,*
42. *Lievrite,*
43. *Dipyre.*

1.—*Mica;* spec. gr. 2.8. Composed of silica 47, alumina 22, oxide of iron 15.5, potash 14.5, oxide of manganese 1.75. Occurs massive, and in tabular hexahedral crystals, of which the primary form is an oblique rhombic prism. The edges of the crystals scratch glass. Its lustre is pearly and metallic; colour, grey, brown, black, greenish, silvery, and golden; with many other glittering appearances. These proceed from the disposition of its plates, which are thin, flexible, elastic. Its elasticity distinguishes it from talc which is not elastic. It melts before the blow-pipe into a greyish-white enamel. With felspar and quartz it forms granite: with quartz it forms mica-slate. It occurs of a reddish-brown colour in felspar, at Kynance Cove, Lizard; and of a grey colour and lamellar texture at St. Dennis, Cornwall; and in beautiful crystallized tables at St. Michael's Mount.

Large thin plates of mica, transparent, and free from spots, are an article of trade in Siberia. It is found in nests imbedded in granite. There it is used for glass.

It is sometimes mixed with the glaze of earthen-ware, through which, from its resisting the heat, it shines like scales of silver or gold.

It is used for inclosing objects for the solar microscope; and instead of glass in the Russian navy.

2.—*Lepidolite;* spec. gr. 2.8; composed of silica 54, alumina 20, potash 18, fluate of lime 4, manganese 3, oxide of iron 1;—colour purple; black, and peach-blossom red ;— occurs in small hexagonal scales, and equiangular six-sided prisms. Translucent; nearly allied to mica. Intumesces before the blowpipe, and melts into a translucent white bead.

It is of a beautiful colour, and frequently cut into snuff-boxes.

3.—*Hornblende ;*—spec. gr. 3.16; consists of silica 42, alumina 12, lime 11, magnesia 2.25, oxide of iron 30, ferruginous manganese 0.25, water 0.25. It occurs massive, and crystallized in single prisms of which the oblique rhomboid is the primary; colour, velvet black ; lustre, shining; opaque.—The massive is generally between greenish and velvet black.

Basaltic Hornblende ;—spec. gr. 3.25,—occurs in six-sided single crystals, of a vitreous lustre;—composed of silica 47, alumina 28, oxide of iron 15, lime 8, magnesia 2, water 0.5. Hornblende is with difficulty reduced to powder, on account of its toughness. When moistened it exhales a bitter smell; and when dipped in hot water, it emits a clay smell. It occurs at Mullion cove; and in the stratified rocks which overlie the granite of St. Just. These rocks are frequently called green-stone. Hornblende mixed with apatite occurs in the slate cliffs below Huel Owls, St. Just.

4.—*Indianite*,—which is sometimes associated with Hornblende,—consists of silica 42.5, alumina 37.5, lime 15, iron 3, with a trace of manganese: colour greyish-white; translucent; lustre, shining. Infusible *per se*.

5.—*Basalt:* Spec. gr. 3. It occurs columnar, and amorphous. Opaque: yields to the knife. It is distributed over the whole globe. Analyses made by Klaproth, on that of Hasenberg; by Kennedy, on that of Staffa; by Kirwan, St. Fond, and Bergman, differ considerably. We give Klaproth's of the prismatic basaltes of Hasenberg, viz: silica 44.5, alumina 16.75, oxide of iron 20, lime 9.5, magnesia 2.25, oxide of manganese 0.12, soda 2.60, water 2; and he found a slight indication of muriatic acid. It is greyish, or raven-black. When fused into a perfect glass, it will resume the stony structure, by slow cooling.

Columnar basaltes, from their regularity and immensity, constitute some of the most astonishing scenes in nature. The hexagonal columns of the Giant's causeway exhibit magnificent specimens.

Basalt, calcined and pulverised, gives mortar the property of hardening under water:—one part of it and two of slackened lime, is the mortar of the great dykes of Holland. Wine bottles have been manufactured with it.

6.—*Wacke*; spec. gr. 2.9, is intermediate between clay and basalt: when it inclines to basalt it contains hornblende and mica. It fuses before the blow-pipe, like basalt into a greenish porous slag, occurs massive, opaque; colour greenish; grey; brown; yields to the knife. We have found an analysis of it in no author.—*Grey Wacke* is composed of pieces of quartz, felspar, silicious schistus, argilla-ceous slate, and mica. The particles are ge-nerally conglutinated by a mass of slaty clay. When the texture is fine grained, the rock constitutes grey wacke slate;—colour, ash, or smoke-grey, without the greenish tinge fre-quent in slate. It glimmers from interspersed scales of mica. It occurs in the parish of Probus, and St. Ewe.

Cape Cornwall forms the northern boundary of Whitsand Bay. It is composed of grey wacke, and transversed by veins of actinolite. A junction is formed on the shore, between the granite of the Land's-end and the grey-wacke of the promontory, by a large vein of metalliferous quartz.*

7.—*Clink-stone*; spec. gr. 2.57; is always found massive, or of an imperfectly slaty structure, and when struck with a hammer, rings with a metallic sound. Its constituent parts are silica 57.25, alumina 25.5, lime 2.75, soda 8.1, oxide of iron 3.25, oxide of manga-

---

* At Por-nanvon cove in Whitsand-bay a stratum of sea-sand and rolled pebbles occurs in the cliff at an elevation of 15 feet above high-water mark.

About a furlong east from the Swan Pool, Falmouth, during a storm in the winter of 1824, the sea encroached upon the cliff, and brought to light in the perpendicular alluvial deposition, several pa-rallel rows, or strata, of rolled quartz pebbles, very considerably above the usual high-water mark.

nese 0.25, water 3, colour, yellowish, dark, green, grey. It generally rests on basalt. Fusible *per se*.

8.—*Clay-slate; Argillite;* spec. gr. 2.7, composed of silica 48.6, alumina 23.6, per-oxide of iron 11.3, magnesia 1.6, oxide of manganese 0.5, potash 4.7, carbon 0.3, water 7.6, sulphur 0.1. Some analysts have found about 4 per cent. of lime, without water, carbon, potash, or manganese. Colour bluish-grey of various shades; sonorous, when struck with a hard body.—Extensively distributed in nature. Slates of soft consistence imbibe water, and decompose by the weather. Seams of quartz, or carbonate of lime, frequently divide slate-beds into rhomboidal compartments. It is the "killas"* of Corn-wall, and the gangue of most of the tin-ores. It frequently contains a mixture of quartz and mica. The brown killas is generally hard, and contains tin more abundantly than copper. The pale-blue generally accompanies a rich vein of copper, and it is the most agreeable to work on, in sinking the shafts, and pursuing discoveries.

The slates of Cornwall form an important article of trade. The quarries lie in the parishes of Tintagel, Lanteglos and St. Teath. From Lady-day to Michaelmas, (it is dangerous for vessels to enter during the winter months,) on an average 100 vessels sail from Tintagel Castle with slates. The cargo averages from 50,000 to 100,000. These are raised in Tintagel cliffs, and North Delabole about half a mile south from the cliffs, in the parish

---

* The miners apply the word "Killas," to clay-slate, miscacious slate, grey wacke-slate, and hornblende-slate if it be soft. Clay-slate of the hardest degree is properly killas.

of Lanteglos. The old Delabole slates, in St.
Teath, about three miles south from Tintagel
cliffs, are shipped at a cove east from Port
Isaac, called Port Garvern.

The cliff slates are of a softer consistence
than those of Delabole. By long exposure to
the air their surface becomes decomposed.
The Delabole slates emit a metallic sound
when struck; resist the action of the weather,
and are distinguished in letters ordering them
from France, by the name of " sky blue
slates."

These quarries employ about 200 men, with
an expenditure of £500, per month.

9.—*Porcelain clay*;—spec. gr. 2.2. Its constituents are silica 52, alumina 47, oxide of
iron 0.38.

In the parish of St. Stephens, about five miles
from St. Austle, on the south side of the granite range, is a rock consisting of a very soft
white felspar basis, obviously formed by the
disintregation of the felspar of granite, very
white and unctuous, through which small
transparent crystals are scattered.* The rock
itself is sent to the potteries in lumps, where
they are ground, and the disintregated matter is exposed to running water, which carries
the fine particles into pits, the floors and walls
of which are of granite, and made water-tight
by Aberthaw lime. (vide *Lime*.) The clay is
transferred from these to " pans" of about 40
feet by 12, and about 14 inches deep. It
remains there from 4 to 8 months. The water having evaporated, the fine white clay

---

* Dr. Ure says, (*Chemical Dictionary*, article " clay,") " the odour
" ascribed to clays breathed upon, is due to the oxide of iron mixed
" with them." The St Stephen's clay contains no oxide of iron, yet
it exhales the argillaceous smell, when breathed on.

is dug out in squares, packed in barrels of from 4 to 5 Cwt. and sent in casks to Charlestown, in the neighbourhood, to be shipped for the potteries, and for bleachers' purposes. A metallic stain either from the water or instruments used, would render the clay unsaleable. The quantity annually exported is from 1200 to 1500 tons, at the rate of £4 per ton. However the price depends much on the demand.

In a space of 8 or 10 acres on the west of St. Agnes' hill porcelain clay is found. It is dug in square pieces and heaved up by the hands from pits. It is also found on the east-side of the hill, on a level with that of the western side, in a compass of from 5 to 6 acres. About a quarter of a mile north from this spot the clay appears again. This clay is sold to the mines for sticking candles and stopping water, at the rate of 20 shillings per ton. Huel Coates adjoining the clay being in granite, the felspar, from its' mealy nature, will not allow the clay to adhere to the side of the holes bored in it for putting down gun-powder, the men are obliged to use tin tubes to preserve it from the water. In that mine clay is found for fire-bricks; it is cut with a shovel and called *pot-growan* by the miners.

The yellow sand upon the north of the hill, which is composed chiefly of silica, is used in making stucco. Upon the clay on the west and north of the hill are found rolled pebbles, similar to those on the sea-shore. The clay must have consolidated before they were deposited, else they would be found imbedded in it. These pebbles frequently contain grains of tin. They are quartz, but the clay below them contains no foreign ingredient. The

hill has been mined in every direction and it
is ascertained that the clay occurs not in strata
but in what were originally pools. White and
yellow sand stand perpendicular side by side
on the north of the hill. The summit of the
hill is 480 feet above the sea, and these sands
and pebbles may be half way.

10.—*Bole;* spec. gr. 1.4, composed of silica
47, alumina 19, magnesia, 6.2, lime 5.4, iron
5.4, water 7.5; but the truth of this analysis
has been doubted. It occurs massive; colour,
yellowish-brown, red, and translucent; pitch-
black and opaque. Fracture perfectly conchoidal; falls to pieces when put into water,
with a crackling noise.

Mountain, or rock-soap, is allied to bole and
lithomarge. It occurs black; adheres strongly
to the tongue; unctuous. It writes, but does
not soil, and is used as a crayon.

11.—*Lithomarge, stone-marrow;*—occurs
friable; snow-white; yellowish, or reddish-
white; soils slightly; feels unctuous, and
gives a shining streak; phosphoresces in the
dark. Its constituents are silica 32, alumina
26.5, oxide of iron 21, muriate of soda 1.5,
water 17. It also occurs *indurated;* spec. gr.
2.44; consisting of silica 45.25, alumina 36.5,
oxide of iron 2.75, water 14, and a trace of
potash. Infusible, phosphoresces, sometimes
emitting an odour like that of nuts. Its colour
is reddish-white; grey; adheres strongly to
the tongue; unctuous.

The friable variety has been found in the
tin and copper veins of Tincroft and Cook's
Kitchen mines.

The indurated species is used in Germany
for polishing serpentine. The chinese mix it
with the root of *viratrum album* for snuff.

12.—*Fuller's earth* ; spec. gr. 1.8, composed of silica 53, alumina 10, oxide of iron 9.75, water 24, muriate of soda 0.10, lime 0.50, magnesia 1.25, and a trace of potash. When good, its colour is greenish-white, or greenish-grey. In water it falls into an impalpable powder, communicating a milky hue to it; but it does not emit a crackling noise like disintregating bole.

It was used by the antients for cleaning both linen and woollen; and before the use of soap it was generally employed on woollen cloth. The alumina it contains gives it this detersive quality, and which, if more than a fifth of the mass, renders it too tenacious to be diffused in water.

13.—*Meionite* ; spec. gr. 2.6, occurs massive, and frequently crystallized in small, splendent, rectangular, four-sided prisms, with tetrahedral pyramids, the angles and edges sometimes truncated. Colour greyish-white ; generally transparent. Constituent parts silica 40.8, alumina 30.6, lime 22.1, soda, and lithia 2.4, oxide of iron 1, carbonic acid 3.1. It fuses easily before the blow-pipe with intumescence into a colourless glass.

14.—*Chiastolite* ; spec. gr. 2.94; occurs always crystallized in greyish-white four-sided prisms, nearly rectangular: in the axis of the prism is perceived a blackish prism, from each angle of which a dark line extends to the corresponding angle of the exterior ; in the outer angles there is a rhomboidal space filled with a dark substance like that of the centre prism. This black matter is clay slate, in which chiastolite is found imbedded. It imparts negative electricity to sealing wax. Before the blow-pipe it fuses into a white enamel. It has not been analysed.

15.—*Saussurite* ; spec. gr. 3.26 ; composed of silica 49, alumina 24, lime 10.5, magnesia 3.75, natron 5.5, oxide of iron 6.5 ;—colour, white ; glaucous or leek-green ; faintly translucent on the edges when fractured ; unctuous. It occurs in rolled pieces, and more generally massive with diallage. It forms a very beautiful rock, called " Diallage-rock," at Coverack Cove, near the Lizard.

16.—*Agalmatolite ; Figure-stone* :—spec. gr. 2.8 ; colour, flesh-red ; greenish, with veins of brown or blue. Occurs massive ; sometimes of a slaty structure. Translucent. It is a variety of soap-stone, and intermediate between steatite and nephrite : it is sufficiently distinguished from steatite, as it contains no magnesia, which is a constituent of steatite. Its principal constituent parts are silica 56, alumina 29, potash 7, lime 2, oxide of iron 1. It fuses before the blow-pipe into a transparent glass.

It is cut in China into little grotesque figures, and chimney ornaments.

17.—*Scapolite* ; spec. gr. 2.6 ; composed of silica 45, alumina 33, lime 17.6, potash 0.5, soda 1.5, oxide of iron and manganese 1. It occurs massive, and aggregated in long oblique, tetrahedral or octahedral prisms. The lateral planes longitudinally striated. Colour grey ; yellowish, or reddish-green ; lustre pearly. It disentregates in the air, and melts before the blow-pipe into a vitreous globule.

18.—*Blaolite* ; spec. gr. 2.6 ; occurs massive, and in granular concretions of a resinous lustre ; composed of silica 48.5 ; alumina 30.25 potash 18, lime 0.75, oxide of iron 1, water 2. Colour, blue ; brownish-green ; brownish-red ; faintly translucent ; frequently unctuous; fusible *per se*, into a white enamel: when pulverized, forms a jelly in acids.

The pale-blue exhibits a chatoyant opalescence, and is cut into small ornaments.

19—*Lythrodes*; spec. gr. 2.5; consisting of silica 44.02, alumina 37.56, soda 8, lime 2.75, oxide of iron 1, water 6.: colour, aurora-red, tinged with greenish or yellowish spots; lustre, resinous. When fresh broken it appears as if spotted with coagulated blood: it is nearly allied to elaolite.

20—*Zeolite*; spec. gr. 2; generally occurs crystallized. The primary form is a cube, which passes into various modifications, as the cube truncated so as to exhibit a parallelopipid; six-sided flat prisms; needle-shaped, diverging, prisms, terminated by four-sided pyramids. It occurs also massive, lamellated, reniform, and stalatitical. Colour, pale whitish-green; silver-white; honey-yellow; red, and blue. Its constituent parts according to Bergmann, are silica 50, alumina 20, lime 8, water 22, with a trace of iron. It is generally opaque; sometimes translucent. It emits a grating sound, not unlike that of burnt bricks, when the finger is drawn across it. It intumesces and foams before the blow-pipe, which is caused by the expulsion of the water from the fused matter. It is soluble, but does not effervesce, in acids. By not effervescing, it is distinguished from stalactites; It has been found in Stehna Gwyn mine, St. Stephens,

21.—*Laumonite*; spec. gr. 2.2;—it is allied to zeolite, but is distinguished from it by suffering disintregation so rapid when exposed to the air, as to fall decomposed like Glauber's Salt, and become opaque: colour, white;

o

sometimes tinged with red. The primary form of its crystals, which occur aggregated, is a rectangular octahedron. Its constituent parts are silica 49, alumina 22, water 17.5, lime 9, carbonic acid 2.5: translucent. It forms a jelly with acids; the lime and alumina are dissolved; while the silica, diffused through the liquid, gives the gelatinous consistence. It intumesces, by the expulsion of the water, before the blow-pipe, and fuses into a blebby glass.

22.—*Mesotype*; spec. gr. 2; consists of silica 50.24, alumina 29.3, lime 9.46, water 10. It occurs pulverulent, fibrous, and crystallized in translucent rhombic prisms, terminated by pyramids. The most common variety is a long four-sided prism, terminated by low four-sided pyramids. It intumesces before the blow-pipe and then vitrifies. It has been found at Stenna Gwyn, St. Stephens; and in the rocks between Botallack and Huel Cock, St Just.

23.—*Stilbite*; spec. gr. 2.5; composed of silica 54.46, alumina 19.70, lime 1.61, soda 15. 09. water 9.83; crystallized in fascicular prisms, of which the edges are replaced; the summits tetrahedral; their pyramidal planes rest on the angles of the column. The acuminated extremity of the crystals shew positive, the attached end, negative electricity. Colour, white; grey; red; translucent: becomes elastic by heating. It intumesces before the blow-pipe.

Specimens crystallized in flat four-sided prisms, with wedge-like summits, have been found in the prehnite vein, in the rocks between Botallack and Huel Cock, St. Just.

24.—*Apophyllite*; *Ichthyophthalmite*; spec. gr. 2.49; exfoliates, froths, and melts into an opaque bead, before the blow-pipe; lustre in its fracture-surface irridescent, resembling that of the eye of a fish; translucent; occ; rs massive and crystallized in square prisms, terminated by pyramids of four rhomboidal planes; sometimes the solid angles of the prism are replaced by triangular planes. Its colour is greyish-white. Composed of silica 51, lime 28, potash 4, water 17. In nitric acid it becomes flaky and gelatinous.

25—*Chabasite;* spec. gr. 2.72; composed of silica 43.38, alumina, 22.66, lime 3.84, soda and potash 9.34, water 21. Its primary form is nearly a cube, the vertical angle 94°. It occurs with 6 of its sides truncated; and also in double six-sided pyramids applied base to base, having the 6 angles at the base, and the 3 angles of each pyramid truncated; colour white; sometimes tinged with a rose colour; and frequently translucent.

26.—*Analcime;* spec. gr. 2.6; occurs massive in small granular concretions; and in aggregated fibres penetrating one another; and cubic crystals, whose solid angles are replaced by three planes. The cube is the primary form. The crystals are translucent; transparent; sometimes opaque; it becomes feebly electric by friction; colour, white, yellowish-red; lustre, pearly, vitreous. The constituent parts are silica 58, alumina 18, soda 10, lime 2, water 8½. Fuses *per se* on charcoal into a transparent glass. A variety occurs in cubes of a flesh-colour, called *sarcolite.*

27.—*Natrolite;* spec. gr. 2.2; occurs in mamillary masses, with zones alternating of yellow, brown, or white; translucent on the edges. It receives its name from the great quantity of natron, or mineral alkali, it contains. Its crystals, which are rare, are acicular, glistening and pearly. Consists of silica 48, alumina 24.25, natron 16.5, water 9, oxide of iron 1.75. Becomes black before the blowpipe, then red, intumesces and melts into a white glass.

28.—*Prehnite*; first brought to Europe in 1783, by Prehn, governor of the cape of Good Hope; spec. gr. 2.8. Its constituents are silica 43.8, alumina 30.33, lime 18.3, oxide of iron 5.66, water 1.83. Occurs massive, and crystallized; the primary form is an oblique four-sided prism, which passes into an oblique four-sided table, irregular eight-sided table, and a broad rectangular four-sided prism.

Specimens of a pale green, which is its general colour, with a shining pearly lustre and translucent, have been found in the slate rocks between Botallack and Huel Cock; when crystallized they generally appear in a circular mass of compressed rhomboids; sometimes approaching to the octahedron; and sometimes globular. It intumesces before the blowpipe, and melts into a blackish-green glass. It does not gelatinize with acids.

29.—*Garnet*.—Precious garnet is of a dark-red falling into blue. The primary form of its crystals a rhomboidal dodecahedron; occurs also in acute octahedral pyramids; and rectangular four-sided prisms; lustre, glistening and splendent. Spec. gr. 4. Consists of silica 39.6, alumina 19.6, black oxide of iron 39.6; oxide of manganese 1.8; It is cut into ring-stones.

Common Garnet; spec. gr. 3.7; composed of silica 38, alumina 20.6, lime 34.6, oxide of iron 10.5. The primary form a dodecahedron with rhombic planes.

Specimens from Botallack, St. Just, occur;
1st, trapezoidal, in micaceous schist; 2d, of a
dark colour, in well defined trapezoidal crystals on compact micaceous schist; 3d, of a
reddish-brown, in rhomboidal dodecahedrons,
with some of the edges truncated, together
with precious garnet. Some of the crystals
occur twenty-four-sided. At the junction of
the granite and clay-slate near Morna cove
garnets occur. Most of the common garnets
fuse into a blackish, or greenish glass. Coarse
garnets are used as emery for polishing
metals.

30.—*Allochroite*; spec. gr. 3.5; occurs massive; opaque; colour grey; yellowish-red. It
consists of silica 35, lime 30.5, oxide of iron
17, alumina 8, carbonate of lime 6, oxide of
manganese 3.5. It sometimes accompanies
brown garnet; and is by some writers rec-
koned among the garnets. It gives sparks
with steel. It is fusible *per se*, and with a
flux of phosphate of soda it passes through a
beautiful gradation of colours.

31.—*Sodalite*; spec. gr. 2.37; occurs massive; and crystallized in garnet, or rhomboidal,
dodecahedrons; colour a light or bluish
green; translucent; infusible *per se*; with
borax before the blowpipe it gives a colourless transparent glass. The constituent parts
are silica 38.5, alumina 27.4, lime 2, oxide of
iron 1, muriatic acid 3, soda 25.5.

32.—*Pyrope*; spec. gr. 3.9; occurs granular,
and never crystallized; it is of a fine or blood-
red colour, which is owing to chromic acid;
lustre, vitreous;—composed of silica 40,
alumina 28.5, magnesia 10, lime 3.5, oxide of
iron 16.5, oxide of manganese 0.25, oxide of
chrome 2. It appears yellowish by trans-

o 3

mitted light; splendent; transparent; refracts double.

Its magnesia distinguishes it from precious garnet:—it is valued as a gem in jewellery.

33.—*Hauyne; Latialite,* from antient Latium where it was first found; spec. gr. 2.7; constituent parts, silica 30, alumina 15, sulphuric acid 12, lime 13.5, potash 11, oxide of iron 1. Occurs granular imbedded in lava; sometimes crystallized in a double four-sided pyramid, variously truncated and oblique; brilliant; transparent; lustre, vitreous; colour, blue of various shades. The opaque varieties are indigo-blue; the transparent and translucent, bluish-green. With difficulty fusible *per se* into an opaque vesicular bead.

34.—*Melanite;* spec. gr. 3.73; consists of silica 35.5, lime 32.5, oxide of iron 25.25, alumina 6, oxide of manganese 0.4; occurs in rough roundish grains, and crystallized in a shining rhomboidal dodecahedron, truncated on the edges. Colour, velvet black; opaque; resinous. Fuses *per se* into a brilliant glass globule. It is considered as a variety of garnet.

35.—*Cinnamon-stone;* spec. gr. 3.53; composed of silica 38.8, alumina 21.2, lime 31.25, oxide of iron 6.5; found in some rivers in Ceylon in rolled pieces; lustre, splendent; transparent; colour, blood-red; hyacinthine-red; orange-yellow:—melts before the blowpipe with ebullition into a brownish-black enamel. It is cut as a precious stone.

36.—*Leucite; white garnet;* spec. gr. 2.5; constituent parts, silica 56, alumina 20, potash 20, lime 2;—it is the first mineral in which potash was discovered; translucent; refracts single; colour, a dull white; lustre, vitreous;

occurs in rolled pieces in lava:—primary form
of its crystals a cube, or rhomboidal dodecahedron; the varieties found are generally
polyhedrons. Its powder gives a green colour
to the syrup of violets. It fuses with borax
before the blow-pipe into a transparent glass.
A green variety occurs, which is called *volcanic chrysolite;* and a brown, called *volcanic
hyacinth.* It is cut into ring-stones.

37.—*Tourmaline;* spec. gr. 3; first discovered in 1717. Its constituents are silica 42,
alumina 40, soda 10, oxide of manganese and
iron 7. The primary form is an obtuse rhomboid; generally occurs in three or six-sided
prisms, with four-sided summits, the lateral
edges frequently bevelled, which forms a nine
sided prism, and the edges of the bevelment
when truncated form a twelve-sided prism.
The lateral planes are generally cylindrical
convex, deeply and longitudinally striated.
Splendent. Refracts double. It is remarkable
for its primitive and permanent electricity,
and electric polarity, perfectly analagous to
magnetism. It becomes electrified by gentle
heat alone, without friction. It is sometimes
transparent; sometimes opaque. Colour,
green, blue, brown, black, red.

Black tourmaline occurs in Saint Just.
Brownish-black specimens are found in compact radiating fasciculi in the granite of
Land's End; and in Roach Rock; it occurs
of a yellowish-brown, in St. Ewe. Red tourmaline, called *Rubellite,* occurs in indistinct
aggregated crystals. Fuses before the blow-
pipe with intumescence. Tourmaline is frequently cut as a jewel.

38.—*Schorl;*—named from the village
Schorlaw, in Saxony, where it was discovered,

The old Cornish name for it is "Cockle." Spec. gr. 3.3. Its constituent parts are silica 36.75, alumina 34.5, oxide of iron 21, magnesia 0.2, potash 0, and a trace of manganese. It is a variety of rhomboidal tourmaline; it exhibits the same electrical properties as tourmaline. It occurs crystallized in prisms closely aggregated, opaque in the mass, long, with many deep longitudinal striæ running parallel; the ends of the prisms smooth. Colour velvet-black; vitreous.

It occurs in tin veins, and beneath the Loggan-rock, near the Land's End. Some specimens have been found at Roscommon cliff, crystallized in minute prisms, which are white and transparent. The prevailing colour of St. Just schorl is bottle-green. There, it occurs in aggregated divergent crystals; diverging, radiated, of a dark-brown colour, with apatite, and in white quartz. About a mile beyond Knill's Mausoleum, near St. Ives, on the left side of the road there is a wall entirely of schorl. Schorl and quartz constitute Roach Rock. Fusible *per se.*

39.—*Epidote ; Pistacite ;* spec. gr. 3.45— composed of silica 37, alumina 21, lime 15, oxide of iron 24; oxide of manganese 1.5, water 1.5 :—occurs massive, and crystallized in an oblique four-sided prism, which is the primary form; its usual modifications, a very oblique four-sided prism bevelled on the extremities; truncated on the edges, and truncated on the obtuse lateral edges, and doubly acuminated on the extremities by four planes; the lateral planes longitudinally striated; lustre, splendent; colour pistachio-green, which passes into deeper shades. Fusible *per se,* into a black scoria. It has been found in do na ci; St. Just; and at the junction of the granite, and clay slate near Morna Cove.

40.—*Zoisite*; spec. gr. 3.3; considered by some as a variety of epidote;—consists of silica 42, alumina 29, lime 21; oxide of iron 3. It occurs massive, of a reddish-white, spotted with pale peach-blossom red; and crystallized in oblique four-sided prisms, their obtuse angles being rounded. The crystals are deeply striated longitudinally, and exhibit a reed-like form; colour, grey; translucent; of a pearly lustre. Fuses before the blow-pipe into a vitreous scoria; with borax it intumesces and melts into a diaphonous glass.

41.—*Axinite*; *thummerstone*, from Thum in Saxony where it was discovered; spec. gr. 3.26. Its constituent parts are silica 44, alumina 18, lime 19, oxide of iron 14, oxide of manganese 4. It occurs sometimes massive; but most generally in axe-form crystals, which are rhomboidal parallelopipids, the two opposite angles wanting, and a small face in their place, striated longitudinally; the edges of the crystals are sharp; translucent; of a violet colour; hence it is sometimes called *violet schort*. Their usual colour is a clove-brown; lustre, splendent; translucent. The primary form is a rectangular prism, whose base is a parallelogram. The most usual variety is a flat rhomboidal parallelopipid.

It has been found in Botallack; Le Mona cave, St. Burien; at Trewellard a little north of Botallack it was first discovered in most beautifully crystallized specimens, scarcely inferior to those brought from Dauphiny. Fine specimens have also been found in the slaty hornblende-rocks of Roscommon cliffs, of a light grey and violet colour; from translucent to transparent; crystallized in an oblique rhomboidal table: some have occured in prisms, It froths before the blow-pipe and melts into a dark-green glass.

42.—*Lievrite*; *Yenite*; spec. gr. 3.8 ; composed of silica 30, lime 14.8, oxide of iron 49, alumina 1, oxide of manganese 2;—occurs amorphous; and crystallized in brilliant rectangular four-sided prisms; colour, blackish-green; opaque; fuses before the blow-pipe with borax into a dark glass. It is soluble in muriatic acid.

43.—*Dipyre*; spec. gr. 2.7; constituents, silica 60, alumina 24, lime 10, water 2; occurs in small splendent fascicular crystals, of which the primary form is an hexahedron; their colour greyish-white, or reddish-white; translucent; lustre, vitreous; very frangible. It fuses with intumescence before the blow-pipe, becomes white and then melts into a colourless blebby glass; it phosphoresces on coals.

Per-silicious minerals are those which contain silica in a proportion of more than 60 per cent.

1. Potter's clay,	22. Horn-stone,
2. Cimolite,	23. Turkey-hone,
3. Quartz,	24. Wood-stone,
4. Amethyst,	25. Jasper,
5. Aventurine,	26. Heliotrope,
6. Prase,	27. Pitch-stone,
7. Chrysoprase,	28. Pearl-stone,
8. Opal,	29. Pumice,
9. Hydrophane,	30. Polishing-slate,
10. Hyalite,	31. Obsidian,
11. Menilite,	32. Felspar,
12. Calcedony,	33. Gneiss,
13. Cacholony,	34. Amazon-stone,
14. Onyx,	35. Labradore-felspar,
15. Plasma,	36. Adularia,
16. Carnelian,	37. Bergmanite,
17. Sarde,	38. Spodumene,
18. Cat's eye,	39. Silicious-sinter,
19. Agate,	40. Float-stone,
20. Flint,	41. Sphragide,
21. Lydian-stone,	42. Tripoli.

1.—Potter's-clay;—Plastic-clay; spec. gr. 2; consists of silica 63, alumina 37; another analysis makes, silica 51, alumina 25, lime 3, with a trace of manganese and some water. It feels unctuous; has a great affinity for water; adheres strongly to the tongue; acquires such solidity as to be infusible in the porcelain furnace; it remains white in a strong heat; this distinguishes it from common clay used for coarse earthen-ware. Colour, greenish, or yellowish-white, or bluish-grey.—It is often necessary to mix sand with it to make *tiles*, as by this means they vitrify the sooner, and absorb less moisture. Earthen-ware, bricks, crucibles, and tobacco-pipes are made of it. *Fire-bricks* are those which contain but little silica, else their being exposed to the action of the fire would cause them to vitrify.

2.—*Cimolite*; spec. gr. 2; is nearly allied to fuller's earth, and is used still by the inhabitants of the island Argentaria for the purposes to which it was antiently applied. Triturated with water it forms a pappy mass: 100 grains give three ounces of water the consistence and appearance of cream. Ground with water, and applied to silk and woollen, greased with oil of almonds, the oil is completely discharged by a slight washing, without injury to the colour. These properties, superior to that of our best fuller's earth, are attributed to the minutely divided state of the silica, and its intimate combination with the alumina. Its constituents are silica 63, alumina 23, oxide of iron 1.25, water 12.

3.—*Quartz*; spec. gr. 2.6; consists of silica 98, alumina 1.5, oxide of iron 0.5. It strikes fire with steel, and is harder than glass. It is only acted on by the fluoric acid. It is translucent; transparent. The primary form of its crystals is a rhomboidal parallelopipid, nearly a cube. The most common variety is a dodecahedron, composed of six-sided pyramids. The vesicular variety is the *Buhr-stone*,* found in France, and used for mill-stones.

* Buhr-stone is supposed to be the siliceous skeleton of a lime-stone, the quartz being deprived of its lime; there remains only a porous mass, very hard, and containing in its cavities a clay-marle. (*Annals of Philosophy*, March, 1819.)

The most transparent quartz-crystals of Britain are found in the slate quarries in Tintagel cliffs, on the north east of Cornwall. There are three quarries; (see *clay-slate ;*) but the crystals have been found only in the cliffs; and not in Delabole quarries, as erroneously stated by writers. (See *rutile.*)

In the beginning of July 1825, a brilliant assemblage of these crystals was shown to the author, in the ware-house of Messrs. Rosvear and Slogget, Boscastle, which lies about 4 miles east from Tintagel cliffs. There were more than 1000, weighing about 3 cwt. and were chiefly sold to Mr. Tregoning, at Truro.

They occur in nests in the slate-stone : imbedded in a yellowish-white clay, like mud ; and sometimes as black as wet soot. The whitish-yellow fluid is decomposed adularia, many perfect crystals of which are found adhering to the quartz; the black matter is decomposed slate-stone,—(manganese?) Although valued by mineralogists, they are not much welcomed by the quarry-men, as the stone about them is always deteriorated.

The two pyramids joined without an intervening column are rare; as are also those crystals with the pyramids complete at both ends. Specimens of both are lying before the author, one was found in Perranzabuloe cliffs, the other in Tintagel cliffs. The primary rhomboid has been found in a porphyritic rock, near the swan-pool. Radiated quartz has been found near St. Day ; and cubic quartz in Carhayes. Malachite quartz occurs in Huel Alfred. Black-quartz in brilliant minute crystals, and also in large ones sometimes perfectly terminated at both ends has been found in Little Bounds Mine, St. Just. Brown quartz, in

long transparent crystals, in Trewellard.
Amethystine quartz is plentiful in Bosavern
mills; stalactitic quartz, in Botallack, and
Huel Alfred. Crystals inclosing schorl are
found at Roscommon cliff, St. Just; inclosing
chlorite in a moss-like form, and oxide of
iron, at Botallack; inclosing oxide of tin,
and copper, and iron-pyrites, at Huel Diamond. The cube has been found in Huel
Alfred; and cubic quartz, every plane of
which is coated with small rock crystals in
hexahedrals prisms has recently been found in
the United Mines. The mines of St. Agnes
have supplied the finest druses of crystal;
there, varieties, solid, opaque, and crystallized
in six-sided tables, with smooth surfaces have
lately occurred; and also octahedrons and
cubes which are hollow, the quartz appearing
to have been deposited on substances which
gave it figure, and which are now decomposed;
a hollow cube crystal supposed to have been
formed on fluor is in the Royal Institution of
Cornwall; again, solid cubes and octahedrons
occur in St. Agnes. The Cornish crystals
are frequently incrustated with ferruginous
copper, (tile-ore;) sometimes with carbonate
of iron.

Two parts, by weight of silicious earth, and
1½ of carbonate of soda are the essential ingredients of glass.

The carbonic acid and water being expelled
in a strong heat, the alkali and earth become combined. This is fused in clay pots,
which is glass. Crystal glass is from the best
pearl-ash and pounded flint. Window glass
is from sand and kelp. Green bottle glass is
from sea sand and the refuse of the soap-
maker's ley. Oxide of lead promotes the vi-

trification; renders the glass more dense and ductile, and susceptible of a higher polish: and increases its refractive power.

Black oxide of manganese improves the whiteness and transparency of glass. It acts on the oxide of iron existing in the materials. Iron, in a low state of oxidation, gives glass a green tinge; at a high degree of oxidation it does not communicate colour. The black oxide of manganese gives a violet colour; it therefore yields its oxygen to the iron which it brings to a high state of oxidation; it, itself, passes to the lower state of oxidation; and each is in that state which does not communicate colour. The basis of gems is pure glass fused with an alkali, with the addition of borax and oxide of lead. Different metallic oxides give different colours, frequently superior to those of gems; but they are much softer and of inferior specific gravity. Iron gives a green; lead, yellow; manganese, purple; cobalt, blue; gold, red.

Glass fused with oxides of tin and lead forms enamel.

4—*Amethyst*—occurs in every shade of violet: sometimes, the lower part of the crystals is nearly colourless, or tinged with green. It consists of silica 98, and a trace of oxide of iron to which it owes its colour. The crystals are six-sided pyramids, and occur always in druses. Beautiful crystallizations of amethystine quartz have been found in Huel Hewas, St. Mewan parish; and in six-sided prisms, of a violet-blue, and clove-brown colour, in St. Cleer, and St. Ewe. Several veins of amethystine quartz have lately been discovered in the Lizard serpentine district. Polgooth and Pedmandrea have also produced fine spesimens. The amethyst crystals are generally more regular than the transparent.

5.—*Aventurine* is a variety of common quartz. It exhibits numerous spots, which glitter like gold, from the intermixture of mica. While experiments were making on glass fluxes at Moreno, near Venice, a portion of gold falling accidentally (*par aventure*) into the mixture, exhibited, on cooling so beautiful a colour, that it was esteemed of sufficient value to be set in rings, vases, and other ornamental articles. "Un ouvrier donna la nom "*d'aventurine* à ce mélange. Les mineralo- "gistes ont appliqué le même nom aux sub- "stances naturelles dont ce produit de l'art "affroit un imitation apparente." (*Haüy*, Tom. II. p. 422.)

6.—*Prase.* Its constituent parts are silica 98.5, alumina and magnesia 0.5, oxide of iron 1.—It is a mixture of quartz and actinolite.—Occurs massive, and crystallized in hexahedral prisms with six-sided pyramids; colour, bluish, or leek-green. Translucent. It occurs in Huel Bellon, St. Just. It is polished as an ornamental stone.

7.—*Chrysoprase*—consists of silica 96.16, alumina 0.83, oxide of iron 0.08, oxide of nickel 1.—occurs massive; translucent; colour, apple-green. It is considered by some mineralogists as a variety of calcedony. It is used in jewellery.

8.—*Opal; precious opal;* spec. gr. 2.1; composed of silica 90, water 10.—It is of a milk-white colour inclining to blue; and when held between the eye and the light appears pale wine-yellow. In its play of colours it exhibits blue, green, yellow, red;—the rarest and most beautiful colour is red. It appears

...advantage in water. It occurs always amorphous; frequently hydrophanous. It is highly valued in jewellery; and is cut into neck-laces, ear-pendants, ring-stones, and other ornaments.

It is cut en cabuchon, i.e. into a convex form, which shews its rich play of colour with great effect. It is polished on a leaden wheel, with tripoli and water; tin-ashes on a piece of chamois leather gives it perfect lustre. A black case sets it off to the greatest advantage.

Common opal, semi-opal, consists of silica 93.5, oxide of iron 1, water 5. It does not possess the effulgence of colours of precious opal. It is greyish, greenish, yellowish, or milk-white; semi-transparent. It has been found in the metalliferous veins of High Rosewarne mine; and of a greenish-white, and chesnut-brown, in Trugoe mine, St. Columb. Yellowish specimens exhibiting a play of red light have been found in Huelapinster, St. Day. It occurs in St. Just, varying from white to grey; yellowish brown and black; and sometimes of a bright-yellow, both translucent and opaque. The most translucent reflect the red ray in a good light. It frequently passes imperceptibly into red or brown jasper; sometimes it is minutely disseminated through porphyry, of which pieces are polished into snuff-boxes, &c.

Fire-opal; spec. gr. 2.12. It is composed of silica 92, water 7.75, oxide of iron 0.25. It is completely transparent; and of a hyacinth-red, or yellow colour. It has been found in High Rosewarne mine, St. Just, and Huel Gorland.

2. Hydrophane; a variety of opal; receives its name from becoming transparent when put

into water, and losing its colour and opacity, which it recovers when dry. From its porous texture, it absorbs the water, which must be pure, and the stone must be withdrawn whenever it has acquired full transparency, else by absorbing earthy particles it will lose its distinguishing property and remain opaque. It also absorbs melted wax, and becomes transparent when heated; it is then called *Pyrophane*.

10.—*Hyalite*; spec. gr. 2.2; consists of silica 92, water 6.33, and a trace of alumina. Colour, greyish, or yellowish-white. It resembles gum-arabic. It is not unlike topaz, but not so hard. It is polished as an ornamental stone.

11.—*Menilite*, so called from Menil Montagne, near Paris; spec. gr. 2.17. It is composed of silica 85.5, alumina 1, lime 0.5, oxide of iron 0.5, water and carbonaceous matter 11. It is allied to semi-opal; colour, grey, brown; lustre, vitreous. The grey variety occurs, tuberose, imbedded in clay-slate; and the brown in adhesive slate, like flint in chalk, near Paris.

12.—*Calcedony*; spec. gr. 2.6. Its constituents, according to Bergmann, are silica 84, alumina 16. By other analysts it is regarded as pure silica, with a small portion of water. Its colour is white, grey, yellow. Blackish-brown calcedony, held up to the light, appears blood-red. It occurs stalactitical, botryoidal, in nodules, and massive. Translucent. Infusible. Harder and tougher than flint.

Fine stalactitical specimens, about forty years ago, were found in Trevascus mine, in Gwinear, nearly opaque, and colourless. They resembled an agglutinated mass of cylindrical bones of small birds; hence, it has been called *skeleton calcedony*.

This mineral has also been found in Huel Alfred, and in Pednandrea mine. That from the latter occurred in blue stalactites, greedy of water; botryoidal, inclosing clorophane. It has lately been found botryoidal in Botallack mine, and incrusting quartz, in Boscagel Downs; and accompanying schorl in the Bunny, St. Just.

13.—*Cacholong*; spec. gr. 2.2; is calcedony of a greater, and internally of a pearly lustre. Milk-white; and opaque.

14.—*Onyx*—is a variety of calcedony; it exhibits alternate layers of brown, black, and opaque white, resembling the colours which sometimes appear on the nail of the finger. When the layers are red and white, it is called *sardonyx*.

15.—*Plasma*; spec. gr. 2.5; consists of silica 96,75, alumina 0.25, oxide of iron 0.5. Colour between grass and leek green, marked with yellow dots, and white spots. Translucent. Infusible *per se*.

Most of the specimens have been found among the ruins of Rome. It was considered by the Romans as a gem, and cut into ornaments. It has been known, for centuries, in Italy under the name of plasma. It was hard as calcedony. Some mineralogists attribute its colour to chlorite.

16.—*Carnelian*; spec. gr. 2.6; composed of silica 94, alumina 3.5, oxide of iron 0.75. Semitransparent; lustre, glistening; considered by some as a subspecies of calcedony.— " It is evident that it once was in a fluid state, " and slowly exuded from its matrix. It is " found hanging in the sides of cavities, and

" seems to have hardened as it sweated out,
" so that the string is incrusted with little ex-
" crescences which have been the end of a
" drop. These icicles often dip into a mass
" of semitransparent calcedony, as if it had
" been fluid, and they can be traced through
" it without mixing with it." (*Black.*)

Nodules of a blackish, or greyish colour,
found in the channels of torrents, in the East
Indies, are exposed for some weeks to the sun,
and then exposed to heat in earthen pots,
whence proceed the lively colours for which
they are valued in jewellery.

Both white and red carnelians occur on the
Looe-Bar, Helstone.

17.—*Sardé* is a variety of carnelian; it displays an agreeable and rich reddish-brown;
but, when held between the eye and the light,
it appears of a deep blood-red colour.

18.—*Cat's eye*; spec. gr. 2.64; consists of
silica 95, alumina 1.75, lime 1.8, oxide of iron
0.25. From an interspersion of white fibres,
it possesses a peculiar play of light; and when
properly cut it reflects a yellowish-lustre like
the eye of a cat in the dark: from this beautiful opalescence it is emphatically called by
the French " chatoyant."

It is found in Ceylon, and is valued as a
precious stone.

19.—*Agate.* The basis of this stone is calcedony, blended with carnelian, amethyst,
opal, heliotrope, jasper, and quartz. It owes
its transparency to quartz. Its general appearance approaches nearest to that of calcedony. Sometimes two, sometimes more than
three constituents occur in the same stone,
which is *Ribbon agate*. Of this *Brecciated
agate* is a beautiful variety. *Fortification*

agate, when polished, exhibits parallel zigzag lines resembling plans of art. Those varieties which exhibit arborisation are called *mocha stone*; none of these vegetable appearances are supposed to be cryptogamous plants. Aquatic confervæ retaining their original colour and form, and coated with oxide of iron; moths, lichens, mosses, bitumen, chlorite, and water, have also been found.

Veins of agate occur at Kynan's Cove; and great numbers of agate pebbles are found on the Looe Bar, and Beach from thence to Portleaven, near Helstone. Agate nodules of an irregular coarse surface found in some places plentifully on the shore, are known by the name of *Scotch pebbles*.

This stone is polished into snuff-boxes, seals, cameos, cups, and plates for boxes; handles for sabres and cutlasses were formerly made of it. Agate mortars are valued in chemistry for reducing hard minerals to powder. Agates are artificially coloured by immersion in metallic solutions.

20.—*Flint*; spec. gr. 2.60; is composed of silica 98, lime 0.40, alumina 0.25, oxide of iron 0.25. It is infusible *per se*, but whitens and becomes opaque. It is less hard and less transparent than calcedony. By exposure to air and water it becomes of a yellowish colour, and is called ferruginous flint; such are the flints of gravel beds, which have been rounded by attrition. In chalk it occurs tuberose; it generally occurs massive, of a gray colour, with striped delineations. Fracture conchoidal. It evidently has been in a tough state like glue.

It is used for chemical mortars;—is an ingredient in pottery; when reduced to a fine powder, it is excellent for glass grinding. The yellowish-grey is the best for gun-flints.

The sand-stone variety is called *pudding-stone*, of which the most beautiful are found near St. Alban's, Hertfordshire. These stones consist generally of roundish flint pebbles, variously coloured, conglomerated by quartz, hornstone, or jasper. They take a fine polish.

Pudding-stone composed of fragments of grey-wacke and quartz occurs near the Dennis Creek, Helford river.

21.—*Lydian-stone* ; *Lapis Lydius* ; spec. gr. 2.6 ; occurs massive, and in rolled pieces ; colour, greyish, or velvet-black, traversed by quartz veins. It is not so hard as flint. It is sometimes used as a *touch-stone* for ascertaining the purity of gold and silver.

22.—*Hornstone* ; *Petro-silex* ; spec. gr. 2.6, consists of silica 98.25, alumina 0.75, oxide of iron 0.50 ; the analysis of a softer stone, silica 71.8, alumina 15.3, protoxide of iron 9.3, and a trace of lime :—colour, grey, red, green. It is difficult to distinguish it from compact felspar; felspar is fusible ; hornstone is not.—It forms the base of hornstone porphyry.

The basis of porphyry is sometimes clay-stone ; sometimes hornstone ; sometimes compact felspar, obsidian, pearlstone, or pitch-stone. The other constituents which are imbedded are commonly quartz, and felspar, sometimes crystallized, sometimes granular.

Hornstone, of a deep blood-red, and also of a brownish-white colour, and of a stalactitical form, occurs in Botallack.

Hornstone porphyry is cut into vases, candle-sticks, &c.

23.—*Turkey-Hone* ; spec. gr. 2.73 ; is composed of silica 72, lime 13, carbonic acid 10, alumina 3. Occurs massive. When polished it is used for sharpening iron and steel instruments. The light-green varieties, from the Levant, are the most valuable. They ought to be kept damp, as heat hardens them. Their powder is used for cutting and polishing metals.

24.—*Wood-stone; Le bois petrifie*; spec. gr. 2.63;—it is found insulated in sandy loam, of a grey, yellowish, or black colour. It is wood converted into hornstone by petrifaction of which the ligneous texture is preserved, and the vegetable matter, by decomposition, removed. It occurs abundantly in ferruginous sand near Woburn, Bedfordshire.

Opal wood is wood penetrated by opal. It is distinguished from petrified wood by its lightness and transparency. It occurs in the shape of branches and stems.

25.—*Jasper.—Egyptian Jasper*; spec. gr. 2.63; consists of silica 75, alumina 15, magnesia 5;—colour, red, brown, &c. Opaque; infusible per se. It is found in great abundance, with masses of petrified palm, &c. in the eastward of Grand Cairo.

Striped Jasper—sometimes constitutes hills. It is of a grey, green, yellow, or red colour; several colours always appear together in stripes. It takes a fine polish.

Porcelain Jasper; spec. gr. 2.5; is supposed to have been a slate clay hardened by the combustion of subterraneous coal mines. It frequently presents brick-red vegetable impressions. Opaque. Composed of silica 60.75, alumina 27.25, magnesia 3, oxide of iron 3.5, potash 0.66.

Common Jasper; spec. gr. 2.6; occurs mas

ble; colour, yellow, red, brown; infusible
per se. It occurs of a black colour with brown
iron-stone, and brown hæmatite, near Botallack
Mine; Brown Jasper is found in Trugoe Mine,
St. Columb; blood-red Jasper, in Huel Mag-
dalen Mine, Lanlivery; Huel Unity; Botallack; Huel Spearn; Huel Stennack, and Little Bounds Mines.

Beautiful antique stones of common Jasper
are preserved in collections.

Agate Jasper—Occurs in agate balls in
amygdaloid, always massive; colour, yellowish, or reddish-white.

26.—*Heliotrope; Blood-stone;* spec. gr.
2.69;—is calcedony combined with green
earth: infusible *per se;* colour, dark-green,
interspersed with yellow, or blood-red spots,
which are owing to disseminated Jasper. Its
constituent parts are silica 84, alumina 7.5,
oxide of iron 5. It is called by lapidaries
Oriental Jasper, and is cut into snuffboxes,
seals, &c.

27.—*Pitchstone;* spec. gr. 2.3; consists of
silica 73, alumina 14.5, lime 1, oxide of iron
1, oxide of manganese 0.1, natron 1.76, water
8.5. Colour, green, black, grey, yellow, &c.
lustre, vitreous; fusible *per se.* It passes on
the one hand to obsidian; on the other to
pearl-stone. It occurs massive, hard, and so
frangible, as often to yield to the nail: it is
generally opaque.

28.—*Pearlstone;* spec. gr. 2.29; constituents, silica 75.25, alumina 12, potash 4.5,
oxide of iron 1.6, lime 0.5, water 4.5;—colour, grey, black, red. The surface of its
concretions is smooth and pearly; in their
centre, balls of obsidian frequently occur.
It intumesces before the blow-pipe. It gives

and an argillaceous smell when breathed on. It has been described as a variety of obsidian, or zeolite, under the title of *Volcanic zeolite*.

29.—*Pumice*—is composed of silica 77.5, alumina 17.5, natron and potash 3, iron-sand mixed with manganese 1.75. It swims on water; colour, grey: does not effervesce in acids. It is sometimes porphyritic, i. e. it contains crystals of quartz, felspar, augite, and mica.

It is used for polishing glass, softstones and metals; also by parchment makers, curriers, and hatmakers. It is used by sailors in the Mediterranean for shaving; and in the East, for removing hairs from the skin.

30.—*Polishing-slate*; *Polier*; colour, white, yellow; soils strongly; swims on water; spec. gr. in its dry state, 0.6; when imbued with moisture 1.9. Composed of silica 79, alumina 1, lime 1, oxide of iron 4, water 14. It is used for polishing glass, marbles, and metals. It sometimes includes impressions of leaves.

31.—*Obsidian*; spec. gr. 2.87; consists of silica 78, alumina 10, lime 1, soda 1.6, potash 2, oxide of iron 1: colour velvet-black, green, iso-black, grey; clove-brown; translucent and transparent. It occurs most generally in the neighbourhood of volcanoes. It very much resembles glass; hence, it has been called *vitrified lava*. In Iceland, it is cut into ring-stones, snuff-boxes, &c. In New Spain, and Peru, into mirrors. It has been manufactured into razors, knives, and other sharp instruments; and has been used for pointing arrows and spears.

32.—*Felspar*—" Feld" in German signifies " a field," and also " a compartment," or " regular surface;" thus, felspar is composed of little ... of rhombic, or other figures; ... (spar) is an old miner's word, and signifies a semi-transparent stone of a rhomboidal figure. The most common colour of felspar is flesh-red; sometimes, a bluish-grey; yellowish, milk-white; brownish-yellow. It is rarely blue or green. There are several varieties; and they are composed of the same ingredients, viz. about, silica 68, alumina 15, potash 14.5, oxide of iron 0.5, spec. gr. 2.5. It is vitreous; fusible *per se*. Next to quartz and oxide of iron it is one of the most abundant minerals in nature. The primary form of its crystals is an irregular parallelopipid. The red colour in crystallized felspar, after exposure to a strong heat, disappears; neither has any substance been found by analysis to which that colour can be attributed: it is not owing to iron, because iron stains in the felspar, by the heat which destroys the red colour of the crystal becomes stronger; hence, probably, the red in felspar, may be merely optical.

This mineral forms the basis of certain porphyries, and is a constituent in many of the most important aggregate rocks. It occurs with green talc at the Old Lizard Head; massive, and of a dull white, at Kynan's Cove; and tabulated with crystallized quartz and white mica, at Cleggo cliffs; and in rhomboidal crystals in the slate rocks, near Huel Castle, St. Just.

Granite is composed of felspar, quartz, and mica. Felspar usually forms the base, or principal part, and is greyish-white, shining and opaque, of a rhomboidal shape. The mica is yellowish-grey; semitransparent, composed of hexahedral plates, or lamellæ. It is unctuous. The mica and felspar, then discover a regular shape; the quartz for the most part exhibits none, but incloses them like a cement. The felspar of the Cornish granite is often distinctly crystallized. The granite masses at the Land's End possess a very considerable proportion of felspar, which is distributed through the mass in numerous, large, distinct crystals, the form being that of a flat six-sided prism. The granite, near the Loggan-Stone, extremely beautiful, from its porphyritic appearance, in some places is traversed by veins of red felspar and of black tourmaline, or schorl, crystallized in three-sided prisms. On the west side of the Loggan-Stone is a cavern formed by the decomposition of a vein of granite, the felspar of which assumes a brilliant flesh-red and lilac colour, and frequently by the attrition of the waves surpasses in beauty the serpentine caverns at the Lizard.

Professor Jameson, in his *Mineralogy*, says " The growan of Cornwall appears to contain " principally disintregated *felspar*." Had the distinguished mineralogist written disintregated *granite*, his name would not have honoured our pages. A piece of granite bruised in a mortar will afford a clearer notion of growan* than his description.

33.—*Gneiss* has the same component parts

* In a little pleasing Book,—" *A Guide to Mount's Bay*,"—we find, " Growan, (granite in a state of decomposition,) has been actually applied as a manure and with the best effects; for the reason that *felspar* contains in its composition a considerable proportion of alumina and potash."

" The quantity of granite shipped at Falmouth, during seven years, previous to 1818 was 40,000 tons. It was employed for the works at Chatham, and Waterloo Bridge. 14 cubic feet weigh 1 ton: a block generally weighs from 5 cwt. to 7 tons. It was furnished from the country west from Penryn."

as granite, but the quartz, felspar, and mica are not in a granulated state. It contains mica in greater proportion. It contains also metallic veins.—In some granite in the tin-lodes of Huel Bill, St. Just, the mica predominates over both the quartz and felspar.

34.—*Amazon-stone ;*—green felspar from South America; found in rolled pieces on the banks of the Amazon. It is cut and polished, and sold under the name of Amazon-stone.

35.—*Labradore Felspar ;* spec. gr. 2.6; frequently contains quartz and particles of mica: the quartz is smoke-grey; and the mica blackish-brown, or yellowish-white. On account of its beautiful colour and fine polish, it is cut into ring-stones, and other ornamental articles. The same specimen exhibits different colours, which run imperceptibly into each other. The green approaches that of the pea, apple, and grass. It is lemon-yellow; lazul-blue; of a copper-red, or tompac-grey, and violet. These occur in spots or in stripes.

36.—*Adularia ; Moon-stone ;* spec. gr. 2.5; so called from Mount Adula, in the Grisons, on which it was discovered by Professor Pini, of Milan. It is the purest variety of felspar. It resembles mother-of-pearl. Composed of silica 64, alumina 20, potash 14; lime 2. It melts easily before the blow-pipe. It occurs massive, and crystallized: the primary form is an oblique four-sided prism, with two broad and two narrow lateral planes; this primary form passes into a rectangular four-sided prism, a broad rectangular six-sided prism, and a six-sided table. Some twin crystals occur. The lateral planes are longitudinally striated. When the crystal is viewed in the direction of the broader lateral planes, a beautiful pearly light is sometimes seen. The lustre, splendent; iridescent; refracts double. It occurs at Tintagel, North-east of Cornwall; (see *quartz*;) and in St. Just, crystallised in oblique four-sided prisms bevelled at the extremities on the obtuse lateral edges. It is valued by lapidaries.

37.—*Bergmanite*—belongs to the felspar class. It is greenish, or greenish-white; lustre, intermediate between pearly and resinous: occurs massive: translucent on the edges. Composed of silica 46, alumina 30, potash 28, with small proportions of lime and oxide of iron. It fuses before the blow-pipe into a transparent glass.

38.—*Spodumene*; spec. gr. 3. Consists of silica 64.4, alumina 24.4, lime 3, oxide of iron 2.2, potash 5. Occurs massive; *per se* before the blow-pipe it separates into golden coloured scales, and then is converted into a kind of ash,—*in cineres vertitur*.

39.—*Silicious Sinter*—is deposited in the hot springs of Iceland, in which it is held in a state of solution, from the high temperature, and alkali, of the water. It is light, and generally porous. Infusible *per se*. Its constituent parts are silica 98, alumina 1.5, oxide of iron 0.5. It is also called *silicious stalactites*. Many specimens are brought from the Geyser fountain. *Geyser*, in the Icelandic tongue, signifies "an infuriated madman."

40.—*Float-stone*; spec. gr. 0.49; composed of silica 98, carbonate of lime 2. It is vesicular or porous; colour, yellowish-grey. It swims on water. Infusible *per se*. It has been found at Relistian copper mine, white and of a yellowish-tinge; and Pednandrea.

A specimen from the latter mine, lying before the author, resembles the yellow froth from the recess of a mountain torrent, which had become instantaneously coagulated; it is in some places transparent; in others translucent; and here and there studded with minute cubes of pyrites of iron. Specimens have also been found in Tincroft mine, of an ochreous-brown colour.

41.—*Sphragide; Lemnian earth;* composed of silica 66, alumina 14.5, magnesia 0.25, lime 0.25, soda 3.5, oxide of iron 6, water 8.5. It has hitherto been found only in Stalimene, (Lemnos.) It occurs marbled with rusty spots; colour, yellowish-grey; falls to pieces in water, when air-bubbles are evolved. The Turks are permitted to dig it once a-year, for medicinal purposes: it is cut into slender pieces, and stamped with a seal, amidst solemnities of religion.

42.—*Tripoli;* spec. gr. 2.2; consists of silica 81, alumina 1.5, oxide of iron 8, sulphuric acid 3.45, water 4.55. It was first brought from Tripoli, in Africa. In Derbyshire, it is called *rotten-stone,* but the constituents of the two minerals differ much. It absorbs water, with a noise, during which, air bubbles are expelled. It is used for polishing metals, and stones; combined with red iron-stone, it is employed in polishing optical glasses. It is sometimes used for moulds for small glass figures, and medallions.

BARYTIC MINERALS.

The basis of the earth barytes has been discovered by Sir. H. Davy to be metallic, which he calls *barium*; and the earth is ascertained to consist of 90 per cent. of barium and about 10 of oxygen.

The metal is of a dark-grey colour, with a lustre inferior to that of cast-iron. Considerable force is required to flatten it. It is fusible at a red heat. It sinks immediately in sulphuric acid, though surrounded by globules of gas. Exposed to air it becomes instantly incrusted with barytes. It effervesces violently in water, which becomes a solution of barytes. Barytes occurs only combined with the *carbonic*, and *sulphuric* acid. Being four times heavier than water these minerals are distinguished by their weight. They are a destructive poison.

1.—*Carbonate of barytes*, called also *Wetherite* from Dr. Wethering who first discovered it at Alston-moor, Cumberland, in 1784, and at Anglesark, near Chorley, Lancashire. It consists of carbonic acid 22, barytes 78. It occurs crystallized in double six-sided and double four-sided pyramids; six-sided prisms terminated by a pyramid, with the same number of faces, resembling quartz crystals; and in hexagonal prisms rounded toward the point. It also occurs massive, and stalactitical in globular striated masses. Translucent internally; lustre, glistening: some of the larger crystals are opaque; whitish or yellowish-grey: the primary form is supposed to be a right rectangular prism.

Its powder phosphoresces on glowing coals. Effervesces in diluted nitric acid, and muriatic acid. By its dissolving in nitrous acid it is distinguished from heavy spar and celestine. It is employed for killing rats in Cumberland. Exposed to a strong heat it parts with the carbonic acid, combines with the heat, and becomes, like lime, in some degree soluble in water, and it slacks much quicker and with much more violence than lime.

2.—*Sulphate of barytes*; *Heavy spar* discovered by Scheele, 1774; spec. gr. 4.7, consists of barytes 67, sulphuric acid 33, occurs massive, the specimens of which present frequently a curved lamellar structure.—It occurs also crystallized in octahedrons, six or four-sided prisms, hexangular tables with bevelled edges. The primary form a right rhombic prism. Occurs transparent, white, opaque; yellow, reddish-white, greenish, or bluish. Yields readily to the knife; possesses double refraction. Melts before the blowpipe into a white enamel. It can only be decomposed by potash or charcoal by means of heat. It has been found in Huel Unity, crystallized in flattened four right-sided prisms with hexahedral summits, and crystallized in six-sided tables in the United Mines, Gwennap, and in Ale and Cakes mine.

Barytic earth has a stronger affinity than any other for sulphuric acid, it therefore decomposes all combinations of other earths with that acid. When exposed to heat and to the sun it absorbs light, which it gives out again in the dark.

Barytes changes red vegetable substances to violet or blue, and yellow ones to brown. It forms glass with silica; and it renders oil miscible with water. An excellent water-colour is made from it. Its *white* never changes, and it may be mixed with any colour.

Sulphate of barytes is found nearly pure in various forms, viz. in coarse powder, rounded masses, stalactites, and in crystallizations; which, in some, are lamellar, in others acicular, in others prismatic and pyramidal. The *cawks* and the *bolognian-stone* are sulphates of barytes. It also exists in the state of carbonate, both massive and crystallized.

The sulphate of barytes (from its insolubility) is less deleterious than the carbonate, and is more economical for preparing the muriate, (barytes dissolved in muriatic acid,) for scrofulous and other medicinal purposes.

STRONTITIC MINERALS.

Strontian, so named from Strontian in Argyllshire, where it was first discovered, was analysed by Professor Hope, of Edinburgh, in 1791, and found to be different from carbonate of barytes which it resembled. Its spec. gr. is near to that of barytes. Sir H. Davy discovered that the basis of this earth is a metal, which he has named *strontium*. It is analogous to barium. Exposed to air it becomes strontian. Thrown into water it produces hydrogen gas, and makes the liquid a solution of strontian. The earth consists of strontium 84, oxygen 16.

It occurs combined with the *carbonic* and *sulphuric* acids, forming

Carbonate } of Strontian.
Sulphate }

1.—*Carbonate of Strontian*; spec. gr. 3.66—consists of strontian 61.21, carbonic acid 30.20, water 8.50;—occurs generally in striated acicular hexahedral prisms; of a white colour slightly tinged with green. Translucent. In a strong heat it attacks the crucible, and melts into a glass, resembling crystallized phosphate of lime. Primary form an oblique four-sided prism, bevelled on the extremities; of a glistening lustre.

2.—*Sulphate of Strontian. Celestine.* Colour, frequently a delicate blue;—it occurs also white, grey, yellowish-white, or red; massive, and crystallized. The primary form of its crystals a right rhomboidal prism. The secondary forms are four or six-sided prisms, terminated by two, four or eight-sided summits; occurs also stellated and fibrous; the fibres long and closely adhering and radiated; lustre shining; translucent and opaque. Spec. gr. 3.6, fuses before the blow-pipe into a white opaque, or friable enamel.

Pulverised and thrown on glowing coals it emits red sparks. This happens also before the blow-pipe, when it fuses into an opaque vitreous globule, that falls to powder in the air. The beautiful red fire of the theatres consists of 40 parts dry nitrate of strontian, 13 of finely powdered sulphur, 5 chlorate of potash, 4 sulphuret of antimony.

Pure strontian is of a greyish-white colour, of an acrid taste; when powdered, the dust irritates the nostrils and lungs. Soluble with effervescence, in diluted nitric or muriatic acid. The solution changes vegetable blues to a green. Paper dipped in this solution burns with a purple flame. It is not poisonous.

If strontian be dissolved in alcohol, the spirit will burn with a flame of the colour of carmine.

Q 2

GLUCINE MINERALS.

The earth *glucine* is so called from the property it has of forming, with acids, salts of a sweet taste.

Glucine in its pure state is obtained from the emerald or beryl, by chemical means. It is white; soft; insipid; and adheres to the tongue. Infusible; and insoluble in water; though it may be formed into a ductile paste which is not hardened by heat.

Sir H. Davy, by his researches, has rendered it probable, that this earth has a metallic basis—*glucinum*—combined with oxygen.

Emerald ; spec. gr. 2.7. It is composed of silica 64.5, glucina 13, oxide of chrome 3.25, lime 1.6, water 2. Though silica be the prevailing ingredient, no doubt glucine impresses the predominating character, and to chrome it owes its rich grass-green. It is fusible with difficulty *per se* generally crystallized in six-sided prisms, the lateral planes smooth, the terminal planes rough. Translucent. Causes double refraction. It is one of the softest of the precious stones.

" The eye, after viewing the beautiful co-
" lours of the sapphire, the ruby and topaz,
" reposes with delight on the fresh and ani-
" mating colour of the emerald, the charming
" emblem of the vegetable kingdom."

Beryl; spec. gr. 2.7. It is crystallized like
the emerald : the crystals are long, the lateral
planes longitudinally striated; their terminal
planes smooth, the pyramid being replaced.
It consists of silica 69, alumina 14, glucina 14,
and a trace of iron. It is with difficulty fusible *per se.* It is pale-green, from the absence
of chrome, iron being its colouring matter.
Transparent and translucent. It causes double
refraction. It becomes electric by friction.

Euclase; spec. gr. 2.9 to 3.3. It is so called
from its great refrangibility. It is a rare and
beautiful mineral, from South America. It is
composed of silica 48.32, alumina 30.56, glau-
cina 21.78, oxide of iron 2.22, oxide of tin
0.70. Before the blow-pipe, it loses its transparency, which indicates the presence of water
of crystallization, and then melts into a white
enamel. It is green; blue. The primary
form of its crystals is a rectangular prism, but
it usually occurs in four-sided oblique prisms.
It is always crystallized; the crystals longitudinally striated.

ZIRCON MINERALS.

Zircon—spec. gr.4.3 ;—was first discovered in the *Jargon of Ceylon*, in 1,89.—it has since been found in the jacinth ; colour, grey ; green ; brown. Translucent, refracts double ;—occurs generally in roundish pieces ; and in tetrahedral, or octahedral prisms. The regular form is an octahedron ; but the tetrahedral pyramids are separated by a column. Its constituents are zircon 96, silica 31.5, oxide of iron 0.5. It unites with all the acids, but is not found in nature combined with any. Before the blowpipe it emits a yellowish phosphoric light, but does not melt.

Hyacinth ; spec. gr. 4.6, occurs in angular grains, and crystallized in small rectangular four-sided prisms, more or less truncated and bevelled. Composed of zircon 70, silica 25, oxide of iron 0.5;—colour hyacinth-red; brown. Semitransparent ; refracts double. Lapidaries deprive the dark varieties of their colour by heat, and make them resemble diamond. It is imitated by heating rock-crystal, and putting it into a solution of dragon's blood.

YTTRIOUS MINERALS.

The earth *yttria* was discovered in 1794, by Professor Gadolin, at Ytterby, in Sweden. It occurs as a constituent part of the mineral *Gadolinite*, named from him. Spec. gr. 4. (See page 92.)

Yttria when pure is perfectly white; has neither taste nor smell; with borax it melts into a white glass.

Sir H. Davy says, it consists of inflammable matter, metallic, in its nature; combined with oxygen. Its specific gravity; its forming coloured salts: its property of oxygenizing muriatic acid, and long calcination; its gaining metallization, when treated with potassium in the same way as other earths, warrant such an opinion.

THORINA.

Thorina was discovered by Berzelius, in 1816. It resembles zircon. When washed and dried it is white; and dissolves with effervescence in acids. It combines with avidity with carbonic acid. It fuses with borax before the blow-pipe into a transparent glass.

As the salifiable bases are considered metallic oxides, and as these bodies are divided into alkalies, earths, and metallic oxides; and as the earths are particularly distinguished by the property of being colourless, and of not being reduced by charcoal, without the aid of another metal, thorina is considered as belonging to the earths. Zircon is the earth to which it has the greatest analogy, and they are generally found together.

Thorina differs from zircon: after being heated to redness, it is still capable of being dissolved in acids: sulphate of potash precipitates zircon from solutions containing an excess of acid; but it does not precipitate thorina:—sulphate of thorina yields transparent crystals: while sulphate of zircon, when subjected to evaporation, forms a gelatinous transparent mass, without crystallization.

ALKALINE SALTS.

Alkalies are substances which, combining with acids, either impair their activity, or neutralize it; and by this union they produce salts.

The alkalies are *potash, soda, lithia,* which are termed fixed, because they are not volatilized by a moderate heat; and *ammonia,* which is volatile alkali.

POTASH.

Sir H. Davy has discovered that potash consists of oxygen united with a metallic base —*Potassium*—which of all known substances has the strongest attraction for oxygen; and even to such a degree that the oxides of potassium are more dense than the metal itself.

It resembles quicksilver and is lighter than water; by exposure to oxygen, it become alkali again. Potash consists of potassium about 83, and oxygen 17. It is found combined with the *carbonic* and *nitric* acids.

1.—*Carbonate of potash* is always prepared by incineration of vegetable substances and lixiviation.

2.—*Nitrate of potash ; nitre ; saltpetre.* It occurs as an efflorescence partly in a state of incrustation; partly crystallized on the soil in warm and dry climates, particularly in the East Indies, Spain, and Naples. Grounds frequently trodden by cattle and impregnated by their excrements; walls where putrid animal vapours abound, and drains, afford nitre. It is composed of nitric acid 44, potash 51, water 4. Occurs in capillary crystals. Colour, greyish or yellowish-white; translucent; saline; cooling to the taste.

Nature does not supply nitre in sufficient abundance for the uses to which it is applied. Artificial beds sheltered from the rain but open to a regular current of air are filled with animal substances, remains of vegetables, old mortar, &c. and after a succession of months by occasional watering and stirring, nitre is found in the mass.

Nitre enters into the composition of fluxes, and is extensively used in metallurgy. It is used in dyeing; it promotes the combustion of sulphur in forming its acid. Mixed with salt it preserves meat and gives it a red hue. In medicine it is prescribed a febrifuge and diuretic.

Three parts of nitre, two of subcarbonate of potash, and one of sulphur, form the *fulminating powder ;* a small quantity of which explodes with a loud noise when laid over the fire in a shovel.

If three parts of nitre, one of sulphur, and one of saw-dust be made to cover a piece of base copper in a walnut shell, the powder by a lighted paper will detonate, fuse the metal, and produce a globule of sulphuret without burning the shell.

Gunpowder is composed of 75 parts by weight, of nitre, 16 of charcoal and 9 of sulphur. The sulphur and charcoal of light woods, as it is more pulverable and ground separately are levigated to most impalpable fineness. The nitre is dissolved in water, and the solution mixed with the ingredients in wooden troughs. It is kneaded; then granulated through sieves; then sifted; and lastly by a brisk reciprocating motion, is tossed in shallow horizontal boxes. By granulation a freer passage for flame is admitted among the grains; so that it kindles more readily; and the whole detonation is speedy in proportion to the numerous surfaces of contact.

SODA.

Sir H. Davy discovered that the basis of soda is metallic, which he has called *Sodium*. It resembles potassium in many of its characters; it is of a silvery whiteness, possesses great lustre; and is a conductor of electricity. When heated in oxygen or chlorine, it burns with great brilliancy. When thrown upon water it swims, effervesces, diminishes with agitation, and renders the water a solution of soda.

Pure soda is of a grey colour; of a vitreous fracture; a non-conductor of electricity, and fuses only in a strong heat. It is composed of sodium 75, oxygen 25.

It occurs combined with the *carbonic,*

248

sulphuric, boracic, and muriatic acids, forming

> Carbonate
> Sulphate
> Borate
> Muriate
} of Soda.

1.—*Carbonate of Soda ; Natron ;* is found in Syria, and India, in effervescence on the soil; in Tripoli, in crystalline incrustations, composed of acicular aggregated crystals, exhibiting a striated fracture. This is named Trona, and consists of soda 37, carbonic acid 38, water of crystallization 22.5, sulphate of soda 2.5. It effervesces violently in acids.

Natron is found dissolved in the hot springs of Iceland and Bohemia. It is procured from the lakes of Egypt and Hungary. When pure, it yields soda 22, carbonic acid 16, water 62. The natron lakes of Egypt lie about 33 miles west from the Delta. The lakes of Hungary are four : they are from one to two miles in circumference. In April they become desiccated, the saline effervescence—and crops appear in succession—is gathered until October, when the lakes become filled with water. Their borders are covered with crystalline masses. (See page 126.) In commerce it is known by the name of *barilla*, or soda.

2.—*Sulphate of Soda*—is common in saline mineral springs. It exists in abundance under the surface of the earth in Persia, Russia, Spain, Switzerland, and Bohemia. It sometimes effervesces on walls. It is bitter to the taste. It crystallizes in hexagonal prisms bevelled at the extremities, frequently striated longitudinally. Their water of crystallization is sufficient for aqueous fusion on expo-

sure to heat; they melt when the fire is urged.
The effervescence is of a greyish-white colour. When pure it consists of sulphuric
acid 27, soda 15, water 58. It does not effervesce with acids. *Glauber-Salt* is native sulphate of soda.

3.—*Borate of Soda; Borax.* It consists of
sulphuric acid 24.76, soda 19.24, water 56.
When purified of the iron with which it is
usually tinged, it is used in medicine.

The salt which soda forms with boracic acid
is Borax, in which the alkali is more than triple the quantity necessary to saturate the acid.

Native Borax is principally dug from the
sides and shallow places in a lake in Thibet.
The lake is 20 miles in circumference, and is
supplied by springs from the bottom. It is
likewise found in South America, where it is
used in the fusion of copper-ores. When purified it is white, transparent, affecting the
form of six-sided prisms, terminating in three-
sided pyramids:—exposed to heat it swells,
boils, and loses its water of crystallization;
and becomes an opaque, porous mass; this is
calcined borax. Its constituent parts are boracic acid 34, soda 17, water 47.

Borax is an excellent flux in docimastic operations; and is of the greatest use in analysis
by the blow-pipe. It assists the fusion of
solder, causing it to flow, and keeps the surface
of the metals clean. When the fusion in glass
manufactories is imperfect, a small quantity
of borax assists it:—it is used as an ingredient
in artificial gems.

4.—*Muriate of Soda; Common Salt.* It is
the only combination of sodium and chlorine
known. It crystallizes in cubes. It occurs in
large masses, or in rocks under the earth,

which is called *Rock-salt*. About 156,000 tons of rock-salt are annually raised in Cheshire; and 16,000 tons from the springs at Droit-wick, Worcestershire. The salt mines of Po-land, have sometimes produced 20,000 tons, for one sale; they employ constantly 500 men. In Catalonia, in Spain, there is a mountain, between 4 and 500 feet high, of solid salt, without any foreign ingredient.

The art of extracting salt from water con-sists in evaporation. In this country, a brine composed of sea-water, strengthened by rock-salt, is evaporated in large shallow iron boilers, and the crystallized salt is taken out in baskets. In the southern parts of Europe it is obtained by spontaneous evaporation. To compartments communicating with each other sea-water is admitted; and during the process evaporation is brought to that degree, that a crust of salt is formed on the surface, which the workmen break, and it immediately falls to the bottom. When the quantity is sufficient, it is raked out, and dried; this is *bay-salt*.

Muriate of soda forms about 1-30th part of the waters of the ocean. Spec. gr. 2.14. When pure, it consists of muriatic acid 46.55, soda 53.44.

Salt enters into many processes of the arts. As a mordant it improves certain colours; in melting metals it defends them from the air, and preserves their surface from calcination; it gives greater hardness to soap; it improves the clearness of glass; by being thrown into the oven it forms a glaze for coarse pottery; it furnishes muriatic acid and soda; preserves meat for domestic consumption, and is the daily seasoning of our food.

Soda is used in Hungary for soap; and in Egypt it is eaten with bread.

Soda is generally procured from the ashes of marine plants. Soap is thus made. Barilla, or kelp, coarsely ground is mixed with quick-lime to absorb the carbonic acid, and give it causticity; then the whole is thrown into water. This water impregnated with the caustic alkali is let off, and the barilla, or kelp, again covered with water, which is again let off. This is "Soap boiler's ley." Tallow is boiled in this, and gradually acquires consistence as it saponifies. Soap receives its detergent quality from the alkali, and becomes soluble in water. The tallow softens the sharpness of the alkali, and prevents it from injuring the skin.

Soda, in nature, is always mild; that is, in combination with carbonic acid; and it will not combine with oils to form soap unless it be rendered caustic. The bile of animals contains soda, in a state of causticity, by which it saponifies the oily substances in the stomach, and renders them soluble in the other fluids. Muriate of Soda, or common salt, is supposed to furnish the necessary supply of soda to preserve the bile in an alkaline and antiseptic condition.

LITHIA.

Sir H. Davy has demonstrated by voltaic electricity, that the alkali Lithia, lately discovered by a pupil of Berzelius, has a metallic basis, which he has named *lithium.*

Lithia is composed of lithium 56.5, oxygen 43.5.

Caustic lithia has a burning taste, and is more soluble in hot than in cold water. Heat is evolved during the solution. Exposed to the air it does not attract moisture, but carbonic acid. Carbonate of Lithia constitutes a white powder; it dissolves with great difficulty in cold, and easily in hot water. This solution is decomposed by lime and barytes water.

Carbonate of lithia exposed to a red heat in a platinum crucible attacks the metal; the surface assuming a dark olive-green colour. A little coarse sand and water will restore the crucible to the metallic lustre.

Placed in the voltaic circuit, Sir H. Davy has shown that lithia becomes decomposed with the same phenomena as the other alkalies. It decomposed with bright scintillations, and the reduced metal burned. The particles were similar to sodium. A globule of quicksilver made negative, and brought into contact with the alkaline salt, soon became an amalgam of lithium, and had gained the power of acting on water, with the evolution of hydrogen, and formation of alkali.

AMMONIA, or VOLATILE ALKALI.

Ammonia occurs combined with the *sulphuric*, and *muriatic*, acids, forming

Sulphate }
Muriate   } *of Ammonia.*

1—*Sulphate of Ammonia*—consists of ammonia 40, sulphuric acid 42, water 18. Colour, yellowish-grey, and lemon-yellow. It occurs as an incrustation, and stalactitical. Its taste is acrid and bitter. It is found in lava about Vesuvius and Ætna; in Tuscany, and in a hot spring in Dauphiny.

2.—*Muriate of Ammonia. Sal Ammoniac.* It occurs in small crystals, of which the cube is the primary form; also plumose, fibrous, and in crusts. Colour, whitish-grey; brown; yellowish-green. It is a volcanic production, and is found in the lava of Ætna and Vesuvius. That of Vesuvius consists of muriate of ammonia 99.5 muriate of soda 0.5.

It abounds in Newcastle coal. When triturated with quicklime, it emits a pungent ammoniacal odour. It is not found native sufficient for the uses to which it is applied. It was formerly imported from Egypt, where it is procured by sublimation from soot, produced by burning the dung of camels. It is now abundantly made in Europe.

Ammonia is a transparent, colourless, invisible gas. It has an exceeding pungent smell, known by the old name of *spirits of hartshorn.* An animal plunged in it speedily dies. Being combustible, a taper immersed in it becomes enlarged, before it is extinguished.

If a globule of mercury be placed in a little cavity in a piece of sal ammoniac, and subjected to the voltaic power by two wires, the negative touching the mercury, and the positive the ammonia, the globule is instantly covered with a circulating film; a white smoke rises from it, and its volume enlarges, whilst it shoots out ramifications of a semisolid consistence over the salt.

Whenever the electrization is suspended the crab-like fibres retract towards the central mass, which soon, by the constant formation of white saline films, resumes its pristine globular shape and size.

R

Chlorine and ammonia mixed suddenly become pervaded with a sheet of white flame.

Zinc is the only metal which liquid ammonia oxidizes and then dissolves. The protoxide and peroxide of copper; the oxide of zinc, the oxide of silver; the third and fourth oxides of antimony; the oxide of tellurium; the protoxides of nickel, cobalt, and iron; the peroxide of tin, mercury, gold and platinum, are soluble in liquid ammonia.

Ammonia contains no oxygen.

The alkalies change the purple colour of many vegetables to a green; the reds to a purple; and the yellows to a brown. Purple, which has been reddened by acids, is restored by alkalies.

They are powerful corrosives of animal matter, with which, as well as with oils, they combine, and produce neutrality.

MINERALOGICAL TERMS.

Acicular, long, slender, straight crystals.

Aggregated, signifies when the component parts only adhere together, and may be separated by mechanical means. Granite is an aggregated rock.

Alliacious, the garlick odour of arsenical minerals, when heated or struck. ,

Amorphous, without form.

Anhydrous, without water of crystallization.

Arborescent, ramifying like a tree.

Arseniate, the arsenic acid united with a base, as copper in the arseniate of copper.

Arsenic Acid, 100 parts of it contain 64 of arsenic acid, and 36 of oxygen.

Axis of a Crystal, the lateral planes surround its axis, which is an imaginary line passing down the middle of the prism from the centre of the upper to that of the lower terminal plane.

Base, the substance to which an acid is united. Copper is the base of the arseniate of copper.

Botryoidal, globular forms such as are found in copper, calcedony, &c.

Capillary, hair-like appearances in silver-ore, &c.

Carbon, Charcoal, that which supports, or can support, a red heat.—It forms the basis of several of the combustibles, as coal, bitumen, &c. It forms the base of carbonic acid, which consists of 72 per cent. of carbon, and 28 of oxygen.

Carbonate, a mineral in which carbonic acid is combined with a base, as of lime in the carbonate of lime; of lead in the carbonate of lead, &c.

Chatoyant, the changeable light, like that of the eye of a cat, in some minerals.

Crystallization, this term was originally applied by the antients

R 2

to rock-crystal, or crystallized silica, because they thought, that body was water congealed by cold.

Chromate, a mineral in which the chromic acid is united with a base, as lead in the chromate of lead.

Cube, a solid figure contained under six equal squares. Arseniate of iron is called *Cube-ore*.

Concentric lamellar, if an onion be cut in two, it exhibits a concentric lamellar appearance.

Conchoidal, fragments of sulphur, quartz, &c. have not an even but a conchoidal or shell-like fracture.

Coralloidal, resembling branches of coral.

Cuneiform, wedge-shaped.

Decrepitate, salt when thrown on the fire flies with a crackling noise, or decrepitates. The crystal retains the water with great obstinacy, till nearly red hot, when it tears it asunder with a loud crack.

Dendritic, like the growth of a tree. Native copper is frequently found dendritic.

Dentiform, or dentated, tooth-like.

Disintegrated, it is applied to minerals which fall to pieces without any perceptible chemical action. Disintegrated granite is like what one would bruise in a mortar.

Drusy, signifies the small prominent crystals nearly equal on the surface of a mineral. These crystals are said to be in *druses*, or *groupes*.

Dodecahedron, twelve equal equilateral and equiangular pentagons.

Fasciculated, applies to a number of minute fibres, or acicular crystals in small aggregations, or bundles, as seen frequently on arseniate of copper.

Fistuliform, in round hollow columns. Stalactites occurs fistuliform.

Fluate, a mineral in which the fluoric acid is combined with a base, as with lime in the fluate of lime.

Friable; a mineral, the particles of which from slightly cohering, may be easily crumbled, is friable.

Gangue, the matrix. Silver occurring on carbonate of lime is said to have it for its gangue.

Glance, shining; hence, glance-coal, &c.

Globular distinct concretions, little roundish masses, such as peastone, and öolite.

Hackly, a mineral presenting sharp protruding points.

Hæmatites, blood-red. There are also brown hæmatites, and black hæmatites.

Hepatic, *hepar*, liver-shaped. It is applied either to form, or colour.

Hydrate, containing water. Hydrate of magnesia contains water in a large proportion.

Hydrogen, i. e. generator of water, importing that it is one of the component elements of water. It is obtained by the decomposition of water.

Irisated, applied to a mineral that exhibits the prismatic colours.

Lamellæ, minute thin plates.

Lamellar, when a mineral can be fractured, or cleaved into regular and parallel plates it is lamellar.

Lenticular, crystals nearly flat, and convex above and below, and which resemble a common lens.

Lythophyta, stony plants, as coral.

Meagre, applied to minerals of an earthy texture; chalk is meagre to the touch.

Molybdate, a mineral in which the molybdic acid is combined with a base, as with oxide of lead in the molybdate of lead.

Molybdic acid, 66 of molybdena, and 33 of oxygen.

Muriate, a mineral in which muriatic acid is combined with a base, as with soda in the muriate of soda. Muriatic acid absorbs the vapours which float in the air, and forms with them a white fume.

Nitrate, a mineral in which the nitric acid is combined with a base, as with potash in the nitrate of potash.

Nitric acid, 26 of nitrogen, and 74 of oxygen.

Nodular, irregular globular elevations. Flint is found in nodular masses.

Octahedron, eight equilateral triangles; or two four-sided pyramids base to base.

Oxide, applied to metallic minerals, in which the metal is combined with oxygen, which is less than is sufficient to convert it to an acid.

Oxygen, signifies that which generates acids.

Parallelopiped, a solid whose bounding planes are parallel, two and two; or 6 quadrilateral figures, whereof those which are opposite are parallel.

Pectinated, exhibiting short filaments, or crystals nearly parallel, and equidistant.

Protoxide, the minimum of oxidation.

Peroxide, the maximum of oxidation,

R 3

Porphyritic, signifies containing crystals of quartz, felspar, mica and augite. Porphyry is applied to any stone of a compact argillaceous or silicious ground, containing crystals, or fragments of crystals of felspar. The rocks between St. Agnes and Cliggo point, Cornwall, are porphyritic rocks.

Phosphate, a mineral in which the phosphoric acid is combined with a base, as with iron in the phosphate of iron.

Pyrites, so called from its striking fire with steel.

Prism, prisms have four or more sides surrounding the axis. Common starch always separates into pentagonal and hexagonal columns, or prisms.

Pseudomorphous, minerals exhibiting impressions of the forms peculiar to other crystals.

Reduction, when metals, (tin, for instance,) are heated in contact with charcoal, then oxygen unites with the charcoal, and forms carbonic acid, which flies off in an aëriform state, and the *reduced* metal sinks to the bottom of the furnace.

Rhomboid, is a figure whose opposite sides and angles are equal; it has six planes which are parallel, two and two.

Rhomb, has four equal sides, but not right angles.

Schistose, slaty parallel fragments, uneven and without lustre.

Scopiform, refers to crystals aggregated in little bundles, diverging slightly from a common centre.

Stalactiform, of an icicle shape.

Stellated, when crystals diverge all round a common centre.

Striæ, refers to slight channels observable on the planes of some crystals; these planes are striated.

Sulphate, a mineral in which the sulphuric acid is combined with a base, as lime, in the sulphate of lime.

Sulphuret, a *metallic* mineral in which the metal is combined with sulphur, and the metal not in the oxide but metallic state.

Tabular, crystals nearly flat.

Truncated, signifies when the edge or solid angle of a crystal is wanting.

Tubercular, an uneven surface caused by round elevations, as flint.

Tetrahedron, it has four equal equilateral triangles.

Unctuous, relates to the touch, greasy. Steatite is unctuous.

Vesicular, having small roundish cavities, as lava, pumice, &c.

Vitreous, glassy, minerals having the lustre of glass.

MINERALOGICAL QUESTIONS.

Should any question appear incomplete, it will be understood by referring to the one above.—The number opposite each question denotes in what page of the work its solution may be found.

s

Page

INDEX.

———

T 2

FINIS.

POLYBLANK, PRINTER, HIGH CROSS, TRURO.

www.ingramcontent.com/pod-product-compliance
Lightning Source LLC
LaVergne TN
LVHW012204040326
832903LV00003B/109